I KNOW

I Know

A Practical Guide for Awakening to What's Within and Finding Work-Life Integration

MICHAEL S. SEAVER

Seaver Consulting, LLC

Contents

CONCLUSION

Things are always working out for me.
　　　　　—Esther Hicks

Introduction

The universe began when nothing saw itself in the mirror. ~Tor Nørretranders

In August of 2018, I ended a seven-year relationship and moved out of our home into a small 610-square-foot apartment. The plan was to refocus on myself and my business. As I started to do those things, I was able to regain a much-needed sense of balance and peace.

It was a difficult time, but I felt I was on the right path.

Unfortunately, the things I was striving to accomplish in my business as an executive coach and leadership consultant were not producing the results I expected. By mid-May of 2019, I burned through all of the working capital I had. To take my practice from a one-to-one model to a one-to-many model, I invested resources into creating several high-quality, meticulously designed online classes, webinars, and in-person workshops. My return on those investments did not pay off on the timeline I had anticipated.

I used credit cards more than I ever had, and my finances took a sharp turn for the worse. I reluctantly chose to take out a loan from PayPal to cover expenses.

Eventually, I was late on those payments.

Things felt extremely dire.

I couldn't wrap my mind around why the things I was building were yielding zero monetary returns. The normal sales approaches I tried weren't working. My pipeline mysteriously dried up, and at the same time, the online classes I'd built out weren't selling. As my workshop slots failed to fill up, the coaching clients I was able to attract were disappearing, too. No VIP days. No three- or six-month agreements. No hourly meetings.

I couldn't understand what was happening . . . or why. I made what felt like a powerful, purposeful business decision to transition to a new revenue model. This shift came with higher overhead expenses, and because my new services weren't selling, less revenue was flowing into my business. Everything seemed to be inverting. In years past, I'd been able to provide services with a limited amount of direct expense. But by May, my business had new event and technology costs. It felt deeply challenging because I didn't know how to remedy the situation. I thought I had to be persistent. I had to make it happen.

I had to find a way to get paid.

Despite the pressure, I didn't have the desire to give more time to my podcast, marketing, or anything else. I felt confused, lost, unsure, unsupported, vulnerable, and misaligned. I was also intensely embarrassed and ashamed.

The thing that was hardest for me to accept during that dark time was the feeling of uncomfortable . . . familiarity.

Let me explain. Up to that point in my life, I had—significantly—struggled to connect emotionally, in terms of life philosophy, with my father, Jack, who is also a business owner. My dad is a people-oriented extrovert and Evangelical Christian. A baby boomer with a high school diploma and a colorful wardrobe, he doesn't enjoy traveling internationally but does love catching the 6:00 p.m. news. He tends to hold onto material things and followed his father's life path. I, on the other hand, am a task-oriented Generation Y introvert with an MBA. I identify with Buddhist beliefs, and I love international travel and blue clothing. I don't watch cable. I donate unused material things and broke away from the family business and small-town lifestyle at a young age by moving across the country.

As far as I know, my dad has never made or followed a budget. This has challenged our family quite a bit, especially when my sister Amy and I were young. And there I was, watching my business walk down a nearly identical path, making some of the same mistakes my dad made.

Looking in the mirror and seeing the reflection of the emotions I'd felt throughout life nearly put me over the edge.

I thought, "How am I really any different than Dad? Why am I making the same mistakes? Really smart people surround me, so why have I not been able to learn this lesson?"

I needed a reset, but I didn't know how to accomplish it.

The apartment I rented after leaving my relationship was in one of Phoenix's toughest, poorest neighborhoods. I heard sirens and nearby freeway noises continuously; my complex had 24-hour security. The neighborhood was home to feral cats and loud parties but no restaurants or grocery stores. It brought me a new understanding of the phrase "food desert." The unit had almost no storage, so I chose to donate most of my unneeded belongings. I moved in with one bed, loveseat, TV, and desk. My rented BMW stood out in the parking lot.

I was lying on the bedroom floor with essentially nothing, a surreal experience for me because at previous points in my life, I had enjoyed material wealth. I had owned the two-story 3,000-square-foot house. I had flown in private jets. I had golfed Pebble Beach and St. Andrews.

Yet there I was, on the floor next to do-it-yourself IKEA furniture.

I felt incredible despair. I did not know what to do.

It wasn't for lack of trying, either. I'd carefully feng shui'd the space, gone for walks regularly, and ate alkaline foods. I'd sat with energy healers, trying to uncover a way to turn my luck around in any way, shape, or form. I arrived at this place of being completely fed up. Sick of trying so hard. My thoughts were scattered and questioning, "Why am I doing this? Can I stop? Should I be doing something completely different with my life? Why is it that I'm becoming what I've *not* wanted to become?!"

Lying on the floor in the bedroom, I was surrounded by things that were the antithesis of who I am. My heart is open, abundant, loving, caring, and welcoming. I enjoy serving others yet was surrounded during those months by people who didn't interact with one another. Person-to-person violence was prevalent in that part of the city; no one said hello on the street. My refrigerator was bare, no art on the walls, no desire to be in a romantic relationship, no emotional safety to ask friends to visit. My stepdaughter Aleah was away at college. I was thinking, "Should I be alive? Should I be even here? How could I commit suicide? What would that look like?"

It was my life's darkest moment. I was bawling, shaking, crying.

Then something unusual happened.

Cleopatra, my cat, walked over to me and laid down on my chest.

It is important to understand that Cleo isn't the type of cat that gives anyone—even me—affection. That is not her style; it's not what she does. But for some reason, she came directly to me and lay on my chest purring with a resonance that sent waves of energy through me. I slowly began feeling peace and balance filter through every cell in my body.

At that moment, I heard my inner voice say, "You're going to get through this. Everything will be okay. Your purpose is much bigger than you can currently see. You need to stay."

I had had everything at various points in my life. Trying to re-build—to get back to abundance—wasn't working. The question was, *Do I want to be alive or do I not?*

I was absolutely past the point where I *didn't* want to be on Earth anymore. Yet as I was beginning to choose how I'd leave, Cleo served as the messenger that I needed to stay. I had to uncover a deeper emotional resilience because my life's work, its purpose, was much bigger than what I could see at that moment. The hardship was transpiring for a reason that was meant to help, serve, and support me. I was confronted with my own humanity, my own frailty.

Of course, I questioned this idea: "Why would a cat who was randomly born in rural Minot, North Dakota, show up on my ex-girlfriend's mom's doorstep and save my life this many years later?"

I received Cleopatra in December of 2011 as a Christmas gift. I could not understand why she was given to me as a gift then. Up until 2019, she was rarely affectionate. She was standoffish, independent. She liked to live life her way. I've loved and cared for her but secretly wondered if she'd ever express love more freely.

And then it all started to click. Cleo reminded me how to stay grounded. How to connect life's disparate dots. How our pain becomes our purpose. How obstacles unlock the next level of our life.

Welcome to Your Earth School Curriculum: Class Is Now in Session

That day got me thinking about why all humans seem to have lives that are filled with emotional challenges. Many of the great Buddhist teachers and monks have asked and answered similar questions. The Buddha's teachings, the Four Noble Truths, hold that suffering is a fact of human life, that the root of all suffering is desire, ignorance, and hatred, that it is possible to free oneself from suffering, and that the way to do so is via the Eightfold Path as a means to enlightenment. Why was it that I thought ending this life was somehow going to be more viable than staying and learning from it? I suppose the hard part is we often can't see the path ahead of us even though we would like to.

After my experience on the floor, I read an important book by H. Ronald Hulnick and Mary R. Hulnick entitled *Loyalty to Your Soul*. I began to understand souls choose Earth as a place where they can learn a curriculum. We are here to learn specific emotions to help us become humbler servants of ourselves and others. I found immense value in saying to myself, "I need to stay here. I can learn these lessons. I'm capable of overcoming my fears and doing emotionally difficult things. It's possible my soul chose this curriculum ahead of time."

Not too long after reading that enlightening book, I began using The Pattern app. It presents what I believe to be our unique Earth school curriculum. When I started to connect the dots between the challenge I just experienced and other events in my life, I began to see that all of the hardships I'd experienced had a purpose. Each was teaching me something I would later teach others. I finally understood that someday, my story and learning would inspire others to find the courage to walk through their own pain and into their purpose here on Earth.

When I began thinking about how to uplift others, I realized simply telling my story was a powerful starting point. Sharing what I think about or struggle with emotionally is valuable as it offers psychological safety to anyone who desires to share but is scared to. However, I believe I can offer more. People could use a scripted, well-tested, and proven process to follow to move from a place of loss and fear to one of discovery and creation. When I talk to my clients about how to focus, channel, and usefully direct their stories, I came to understand that a guided journey would be helpful for many. I'm not saying that your life—or anyone's life—is ever scripted. What I *am* saying is that when you, as a coach, leader, or parent, are trying to guide another person to do something for the first time, you will have a more meaningful impact by moving them through an intentional process. They feel safer taking calculated risks knowing they're following a process that has guided others.

That's what we'll do together in this book.

You'll be walked through stories, research, and steps.

I'll help you feel safe to move from believing in something external to yourself to flourishing from a place of inner knowing.

As I tell my story in these pages, through each successive chapter I will be layering in resources and processes to reveal how I am—and all of us can become—awakened. There is a logical sequence of personal ascension we'll explore in three distinct parts to help you release old ways of doing things, discover your astonishing potential, and make new and powerful decisions in your life.

This book is for you if you find yourself on the precipice of change, if there are too many options and you feel unclear about what route to choose. It is for you if you are unwillingly confronted with troubling news and feel paralyzed with fear.

Or perhaps you've been placed in a professional role that you've not filled before and don't know what steps to take to thrive. You feel frustrated that others are reactive and you are unable to motivate them to take aligned action. Finally, this book is for you if you are facilitating cultural change in your organization, but the team isn't embodying the new mores.

I've led a variety of clients through these personal and team transformations, and now I share lessons learned and easy-to-implement practices with you.

Becoming Your Own Engine

I am here to help people become more authentic. To learn through one another. To feel safe in trusting the Earth school curriculum process. Traditionalists (born between 1900–1945) and baby boomers (born between 1946–1963) were raised during the "I believe in something external to myself" time in human history. So, as long as organizations, institutions, and bureaucracies run by these generations are still in power, there will be situations where sharing your authentic journey will be questioned. But that's changing—and fast.

My role is to offer Generation X (born between 1964–1979), Generation Y (born between 1980–1995), and Generation Z (born after 1996) a deeper sense of safety with their own inner knowing, to transition from "I believe" to "I know." In the coming years, all humans will be given the opportunity to accept themselves and the knowledge and wisdom they hold in their own heads, hearts, and souls.

When this occurs, you won't have to attach your identity to a belief structure, organization, or sports team to feel accepted and an integral part of something bigger than yourself. Instead of a railroad car being pulled by an engine, you'll become your *own* engine. You'll be able to shed connections to outdated hierarchies and replace them with affiliation to horizontal networks where all participants are recognized for their uniqueness, journey through life, and soul's work.

Your mantra, if you choose this path, will shift from "I believe in things outside myself" to "I know I already have all the answers." Stepping into "I Know," starts with a three-phase process. With a nod to change consultant William Bridges's

Transition Model, it begins with ending and letting go of old habits. Next, you'll enter a neutral zone of discovery. Finally, new beginnings appear via intentional decisions.[1] This could manifest by instituting an emotional intelligence training or a staff psychologist-type program inside your organization. It may mean you reconsider what you share about yourself with your most trusted confidants . . . and expand it. Perhaps you create an environment as a leader where people feel more comfortable to show up authentically.

I invite you to stop looking to celebrities, athletes, politicians, or professors for answers. They are inspirations, but their paths are theirs . . . not yours to replicate. Instead, invest in yourself by utilizing these processes you can apply to yourself—alone—to find clarity. Recognize your soul family and your soulmates. Begin to see patterns and act on them for maximum benefit. Refocus your energy on actions that will realign you with your curriculum quickly. Accept that your life's challenges are the path. Learn to avoid shying away from and fully embrace hardship, pain, and vulnerability. Connect with your soul's guidance, and avoid letting your ego, rational mind, and physical body lead you down misaligned paths.

Many people believe an external deity, parent, boss, partner, or another person can offer them the right answers to their lives' most pressing questions. The truth is, there is no one right way. Attempting to emulate someone else's choices may not be *your* right way. Instead, your right way is uncovered only by looking within your own soul and awakening the power you find there, not by following in others' footsteps.

With this vision in mind, let's get started.

Part One

Dilemma

Let go of and shed old beliefs, habits, and ways of being

Feelings You're Having: shock, loss, uncertainty, fear

Actions You're Taking: getting irritated easily, complaining often, panic buying, playing the victim, blaming others, hoarding goods, creating stories based on rumors, transmitting negative emotion

Challenges You're Encountering: letting go of the past; releasing old habits, routines, and emotions

Your Focus: on "them"

Ask Yourself: What do I fear? Why? What am I losing? What am I learning? What will remain the same? Who will support me?

To Find Balance, You'll Be Influenced By: facts, data, logical processes

What You Can Communicate to Uplift Others: Share reliable information, set clear expectations, explain the "why," define the process, share the benefits of an approach

Chapter 1: Loss

Don't trade your authenticity for approval. ~Leslie Cassidy

My family wasn't one to celebrate being yourself.

My grandfather Herb and my father wanted all of their children and grandchildren to work for the family lawn maintenance, landscaping, and snow removal business in Montague, Michigan, and do what it was that *they* wanted the family to do—not what we wanted to do. I'm not sure they were aware of any other way. And so I felt like a robot building their business. I remember working hard from sunrise to sunset.

For the entirety of my teenage years and early 20s, I felt stifled.

In 1953, my grandfather launched the family business. Over four decades, his hard work and business savvy led him to become a millionaire. I knew his sacrifice benefitted him immensely. He and my grandmother Esther deserved the abundance. Yet I also knew society was evolving and there were new ways the business could be managed. I didn't believe we could use old hierarchical leadership models any longer. Those command and control methodologies worked beautifully in the '60s, '70s, '80s, and '90s. But they weren't going to work after the year 2000. We needed to align and empower.

I wasn't able to convince anyone that society was evolving. My dad chose to manage the business the same way my grandfather did. I knew there was a transition happening on Earth. I had the inkling of an answer. I genuinely wanted to help the family members who chose not to listen and make the changes that may have set up the business for future prosperity. As a result, the feeling I experienced most was of disregard. Of not being valued. My opinion seemed to not matter, and that feeling was amplified as the business encountered challenges.

We experienced considerable loss.

I understand, of course, that seeing your family business contract and struggle is not the same as suffering the loss of a loved one. What triggers each of us to feel a sense of loss will be different. But many of the emotions remain the same. Pain offers us the opportunity, but it is our choice if or when we align with our curriculum. I believe we come into our lessons when we're ready. Perhaps the pain isn't what's meant for you—but the lesson is—and that just happens to be how it's being delivered. The painful losses and transitions my family endured through those years are now being experienced by my clients both personally and professionally. Any time we experience change—and humans are living in a time of immense change—there is a feeling of loss.

I watched employees go involuntarily. Vacation houses were sold prematurely. Once strong bonds crumbled to animosity. I thought, in my heart of hearts, that I could better the business if my dad would just *listen* to me.

He chose not to.

And he wasn't necessarily wrong during those years.

I was.

It was never my job to save that business. This was beyond challenging for me to accept—nearly impossible for me to accept, in fact—because I knew I had impactful connections, a simpler path forward, a vision for how it could all transpire. The problem? I was trying desperately to do something in opposition to my father's Earth school curriculum. When I realized what I was attempting to do was in opposition to what *he* was here to do, it cemented for me the notion that we all have a curriculum . . . and I wasn't learning mine fast enough.

I was foolishly trying to control, force action, and do something *onto* another person, the same way it had unknowingly been done to me. The same way *I* had felt suppressed, I was then making others in my family feel the same way.

Sometimes, processing your feelings of loss is the only way forward. The first step is to let go.

Learning Our Lessons

I experienced emotion in March, April, May, and June of 2019 at a depth I can't recall experiencing before. Raised on a small farm, I spent my childhood bottling up my feelings. Winters, with their lake effect snowstorms, were particularly isolating and harsh. At the time, we had a wood furnace in our farmhouse, and the job of keeping the wood split and basement stocked belonged to my sister and me. It was a place and time where we were not taught how to feel and express emotions openly, so I was unfamiliar with deep feelings. Emotions were not shared openly in our family. Each of us felt them. It wasn't commonplace to talk in-depth about our day, what made us upset, or what we were proud of. From the time I left at age 23 and moved to Arizona, through age 38, I experienced emotions at only a surface level. The events of May of 2019 taught me to feel emotions at a level 100 times deeper.

It happened through loss and failure. Through my willingness to allow both.

Are *you* allowing for your feelings of loss?

Because of my work, I sense the emotions of those around me quite clearly. I read them through tone of voice, body language, or the words an individual has chosen. What I believe the universe wanted me to do was learn to experience deep loss for myself. It was something I had previously overlooked, repeatedly. In 2008, my wife Kasen left me because I was emotionally unavailable (more on this later). I've been fired from jobs because I refused to play the game. Loved ones passed. The opportunities were there, yet I missed them. I defaulted to "Let me help this person. I'll take this action. I'm a victim of this circumstance," as opposed to being still, going within, and releasing undealt-with emotions.

We desire delivery of the lessons we need to learn to occur softly, but they're not meant to come to us that way each time. The messaging I received in the years leading up to 2019 was increasing in intensity, and *I wasn't hearing it*. I was living out of alignment with my Earth school curriculum. And so, in an emotionally difficult period, I was rapidly realigned with my curriculum. For 38 years it seemed I was *around* it, but not necessarily *on* it. Then in the span of three short months, I was guided back onto the plan through emotions I'd never experienced.

I now look at coaching, workshops, training, and organizational cultural change—and my work as a public speaker and author—so differently than I would have even a year ago. I once saw my work as means to an end. I looked at the production of money as a way to emulate my grandfather and to lift my father out of a difficult place. The acquisition of money was a way to be a protector—to go back to Montague to transform the business and, thus, my extended family. That was the colored lens through which I viewed my work. Now, I more clearly see that each of my family members has their own Earth school curriculum, and it's not my place to interrupt it. It is not my role to deliver their karma.

Today, I see my business as an end unto itself.

Instead of working to make money to transition my family's business to the next generation, I'm living my life's work through Seaver Consulting, LLC. I'm blessed to help people awaken to their true purpose and authentic selves. If I make money, fine. If I don't make money, also fine. What matters is that I, and others, awaken.

That transition from making money to ensure my family's legacy carried forward to committing to my work so I could better society . . . that was a monumental transition for me. My moment with Cleo on the studio apartment floor forced me to believe in what I was doing in a different and much deeper way. I believed, at a mediocre level, in my ability to coach. I knew I was able to make a positive difference in people's lives; I've received so many testimonials and recommendations and have felt gratitude for each. I was able to win one-off clients and projects but didn't believe my methods would go viral in a meaningful way.

In my heart of hearts, I feel as though I never fit in. That in some ways I've been ahead of my time, an old soul who chose to come to Earth to help guide people to more authentic versions of themselves and the next version of Earth. Anti-mainstream in many ways, I tend to be introduced to an alternative idea's benefits before the majority openly accepts them. I believe the human body can heal itself and that like cures like (homeopathy). Yet, I live in a country that prefers treatments that have opposite effects of a condition's symptoms (allopathic). I practice eastern methodologies of well-being and spirituality. I worked as an independent contractor performing short-term assignments in the gig economy before the media reported on it.

Despite this persistent feeling of being apart from others, when I had that experience in May, I finally came to believe something I was creating could improve the lives of people all over the planet.

When the universe puts the exact right people in your path for a reason, and you're confronted with the choice to hide or to grow, it's time to start believing in yourself.

I was struggling with knowing the right path, yet nothing was stopping me from achieving my life's work except for my thoughts, beliefs, and emotions. For as long as I can remember, I've struggled with self-doubt. I've known for years I'd share my story via a book. Part of me thought, "You're not good enough, you're not ready yet, you need to accomplish more." I now know, thanks to reading the Hulnicks' book, that that part of me is my fragile ego.[2] It is my work spiritually to minimize that voice in the back of my head. It is my focus, now, to make sure the part of me that just *knows* takes the lead.

I work daily to squash my ego, self-doubt, and worry. I choose to keep going down this empowering path. The right people are becoming a part of my journey at the right time to make it all happen as it's supposed to. Has this *knowing* ever happened to you?

Trust it. I help people release the fear that they don't know.

You know for a reason.

Loss is a natural, expected, and important piece of every human's pain-to-purpose journey. We must be willing to shed something to make room for new and better things, people, and ideas to manifest.

Collective Loss and Rapid Change

Does it sometimes feel difficult to understand what you are reading or seeing in the media or social media? Perhaps you read or heard something that is the complete opposite of everything that you've previously understood to be true, and you don't know what to believe. It can be very jarring.

There are several psychological principles employed by the media to keep your attention, most of which you may not realize are being used on you. For example, the *mere exposure effect* was identified and reported by researcher Robert Zajonc in 1968. He discovered that being exposed to something or someone over and over again is enough to make you like that thing or that person.[3] The six laws of influence, as identified by Robert Cialdini, are also helpful to be aware of in our era of opinion-based news. The media uses the laws of authority and consistency all the time, for example, when it interviews experts to fit a certain narrative, or when it repeats the same story over and over.[4] The result is we often feel a sense of loss without even realizing we've been unconsciously manipulated to feel it.

Here are examples of rapid change you, or those close to you, may experience:

- People spend decades investing their hard-earned cash into their retirement plans. They save money because they believe retirement is going to happen for them eventually. Then all of a sudden something changes, and they're no longer allowed to retire.
- Or you used to really love watching Tiger Woods play golf, and then his personal and health problems took him away from the sport for years.
- Before coronavirus, you were planning trips to exotic lands. Because of world circumstances during stay-at-home orders, you're no longer allowed to travel.
- Not too long ago, a college degree was the path to financial security. Many of us learned the hard way that this is no longer true. Society has placed significant value on institutions, degrees, and certifications. But entrepreneurship is proving to up-and-coming generations they don't need degrees or certifications. The world's information is available for free online.
- We're learning that some allopathic medicines and procedures do more harm than the good they're intended to. If you bought heavily into this one approach to healthcare, and then it's disproved, what will you do?
- Government corruption is being brought to light. Humans were led to believe the government was a morally

run institution, and now we're learning there's much more happening beneath the surface.

What do you do? Where do you go? How do you shed old beliefs, routines, and habits?

Our Subconscious Set-Point

From birth until age seven, according to Dr. Bruce Lipton, we learn behavioral patterns and form expectations that guide us for the rest of our lives. During these early years, the conscious part of the brain isn't the primary one. Instead, our young brain is operating at a low EEG level, in the theta state. In this state, a child's brain is recording the environment on a subconscious level, creating the subconscious emotions and expectations for the rest of a lifetime.[5] Lipton discovered five brainwave states—delta, theta, alpha, beta, and gamma. After age seven, the conscious part of the brain becomes primary. In this state, beta, the conscious brain, guides us to repeat behaviors learned during times our brains were in theta.

When we experience loss, everything we learned when we were younger we can now question. Why are we living or reliving our parents' belief patterns? Why did my parents teach me this thing if it's no longer true? We've subconsciously learned the way our parents lived life, and that helped us integrate into society. But to be authentic, to become your ideal self, you have to shed what you learned from your parents and walk into your own Earth school curriculum.

The Age of Aquarius

The culprit of all this change? Mother Earth. Earth's magnetic poles move roughly one degree every 72 years; this is the well-observed and documented precession of the Earth.[6] The full precession of the equinox takes 25,700 to 25,800 years, moving one zodiac constellation every 2,160 years (approximately). This means that the sun rises into one constellation before shifting to the next one.[7]

Some people believe November 11, 2011, was the end of the Age of Pisces and the beginning of the Age of Aquarius. The focus of the Piscean Age was on hierarchy, power, and believing in something external to yourself. The focus of the Aquarian Age is networks, decentralized information, and knowing you have answers to life's questions inside yourself. In the wake of this shift between ages, some are fearmongering and defending the way things were done. Amidst times of great change, most human beings typically feel a sense of loss as they mourn the old ways of doing things, old norms, and old predictable patterns. Even good changes invite us to first process the emotions around loss.

Fortunately, many have opened their hearts and minds, embraced a golden age of possibility, and are helping humanity expand. Regardless of what path you choose, the evolution will slowly redistribute power from the hands of the few into the hands of the many. From loss, then, will come limitless exciting new possibilities.

But we cannot pretend the losses won't hurt. We need to process loss before we can create something new.

Dr. Martin Seligman is the former president of the American Psychology Association whose work has spanned 50 years. As the author of 30 books and studies in 350 other publications, he is the founding father, so to speak, of positive psychology.[8] Part of his work involved getting people to understand how their capacity to think about a scenario would become a predictive tool for what would happen around them physically. He realized that to process loss, then, we needed to reconsider our thoughts around the three P's, which he introduced in his 2006 book *Learned Optimism*:[9]

- Personalization: The belief that we are at fault when a loss occurs.
- Pervasiveness: The belief that an event will affect all areas of our life.
- Permanence: The belief that the aftershocks of the loss will last forever.

What Seligman was trying to teach is that our beliefs about how the three P's will affect our lives are simply not true. You are not (always) at fault. An event will not impact every facet of your life. You may carry the lesson of a loss for the rest of your life, it may change your trajectory, but the pain is not permanent. When something perceived as bad happens to us, it is happening to teach us a specific and important lesson, but that circumstance will not last for an extended time. Learn the lesson, honor and release the emotion as it is occurring, and then ascend to your life's next level. In other words, Seligman, this giant in the field of psychology, understood that loss is a short-term event that builds our emotional resilience—preparing us not only for new experiences but a total cosmic paradigm shift in the way we live our lives, do our work, and even parent our children.

Processing Loss Step-By-Step

I invite you to define yourself as a person who endures challenges, overcomes them, and helps others do the same. When you are feeling a sense of loss, don't run from it. It's natural. Step into it.

Here's how:

1. Check in with yourself: Tune into your repetitive thoughts. Ask yourself, "What *exactly* did I lose here?" Be specific. Provide as much detail as possible. Then ask, "What do I fear happening next?" "What will remain the same?" "Who can support me?" It is likely that 95% of your life will remain the same even after you experienced loss.

2. Find emotional safety: Think about what you need to leave behind to return to a place of safety and security. When we lose someone, there's a burial. It's a significant visual marker. By talking through exactly what you've lost and creating a symbolic visual ending, you can help yourself move through the loss and find emotional safety again. Maybe you type an email and send it to yourself. You could donate items to a secondhand store. Or you could write a letter to a parent and place it in a fire.

I attended a men's retreat in mid-July 2018. One of the activities the retreat leader asked us to complete was writing a letter to a parent who we felt was not there for us emotionally. I wrote to my dad. I'll never forget learning that these other men, who had found their own version of success, had essentially the same feelings I did, similar Earth school curriculums. We all have some challenges with a parent, and we all have to leave that behind and love the parent more deeply to ascend.

There's no such thing as a perfect parent. But we are responsible for our adult reparenting of ourselves.

The retreat leader did a wonderful job of making the environment feel safe. All participants were listening carefully and taking notes when we shared our letters with one another. Those small cues made me feel safe to share. That weekend helped me understand that my dad didn't do anything wrong. The act of writing that letter helped me release, accept, and move forward.

3. Share with others: The more we feel heard and appreciated, the better. So set clear expectations about who can help you and how. What did you learn? How can you share your learning with others? Who could benefit the most from hearing your story?

At that men's retreat, I was placed into an environment surrounded by people I didn't know, but I felt a deep sense of trust. I shared more about myself than I ever had before, and it felt incredible. When you share your story with others, do it in a unique way that is important to you.

Can you identify a common theme in the troubles? Seek others who experienced roughly the same circumstance and share your journey with them. Not only will it be cathartic for you, but it'll also be helpful to those near you as they'll feel safe to trust in new ways. You don't have to do this in person. You can share via social media posts, in online support groups, and by offering mentoring to others in a variety of environments on and offline.

4. Take action: What are possible new ways of living that might define the years to come? See this as a creativity zone.

You get to brainstorm new ways of doing the things that matter most to you.

In the 1950s, German physicist W. O. Schumann, who was brought to the United States in the wake of World War II, discovered measurable electromagnetic waves in Earth's atmosphere, now referred to as Schumann resonances.[10] Although these waves are variable, their main frequency is 7.83 Hz. Think of them as Earth's heartbeat. Their impact on the human brain and nervous system is profound. Neuroscientists have discovered that when you are stressed, nervous, or anxious, your body's resonance can be as high as 36+ Hz. When you're experiencing loss, it may help to find ways to lower your body's brain wave and electromagnetic activity via breathing exercises, exploring nature, yoga, meditation, and talking with a loved one. By lowering your body from 36+ Hz closer to 7.83 Hz, you'll feel far more balanced.

Why? Because every atom, molecule, and cell in the human body is comprised of energy. Western societies focus on the physical body, but we're beginning to understand the energies that the human eye can't see, on which the physical body is constructed. Studies show that energy from the electromagnetic frequencies Schumann researched affect satellites, power grids, and telecommunications services. Signs are also pointing to their impact on the five brainwave states, melatonin production, and other human biological processes.

From there, James Clear's *Atomic Habits* is a great book to reference when you think about building new rituals in your life. Clear shows that what people don't do well when they take new action is intentionally saying no to old things from the past. Once you shed stale behaviors, you are free to say yes to things that are in alignment with your curriculum, with who you wish to become. You have to clear your calendar and shape your environment; that's where the real change happens.[11]

5. Practice consistency: Processing loss does require letting go. It also requires staying committed long-term to your new habits.

Habits get formed every day of your life. They are something you have to commit to changing. Undoubtedly, there is a sense of comfort in the past. I used to default to eating sugar and other simple carbs to achieve a feeling of emotional safety. They made me feel better in the moment. When we were young, Amy and I were allowed to eat ice cream and popcorn on Saturday nights. Somehow, I associated the ice cream with happiness, joy, and safety. Perhaps it was because I didn't have to think of my parents fighting, going to school or work the next day, or because there happened to be friends staying with us. To break association meant that I needed to mentally disconnect sugar as being the cause of the feeling of safety. I realized I needed to create new conditions of success and support myself when I wanted to repeat old habits. That means changing how I grocery shop and what food I keep in my home. It also means I remind myself all the ways I'm safe, how I'm blessed, and that the sugar does more harm than good.

The Alchemist by Paulo Coelho contains the powerful reminder, "When we least expect it, life sets us a challenge to test our courage and willingness to change; at such a moment, there is no point in pretending that nothing has happened or in saying that we are not yet ready. The challenge will not wait. Life does not look back."[12]

In this human life, each of us is on our own hero's journey, a storytelling framework defined by the great Joseph Campbell in his book *The Hero with a Thousand Faces*.[13] We cannot avoid difficult circumstances. The good news is that these transitions are not about becoming someone "better" but about finally allowing yourself to become who you've always wanted to share. It's relaxing into your truth. The blocks in your path—the ones that make you want to turn around—are moving you closer to and making the journey clearer. The path to this authentic place is paved with, well, everything—the good *and* the bad.

With loss.

"Let everything happen to you: beauty and terror," the poet Rainer Maria Rilke wrote. "Just keep going. No feeling is final."

Who Will Support You?

Have you ever met someone and felt an instant connection that you couldn't explain? Maybe you've just met someone, yet you feel like you've known them forever? Or you can sense what's going to come out of their mouth before they say it? These people might be in your soul family. I don't believe we come to Earth to learn our curriculum alone. Instead, I think each of us is connected to a group of other souls. They are the people we feel most comfortable or in harmony with, the ones we recognize and connect with quickly. People from our designated soul groups have chosen to be part of our learning journey on Earth or to come here with us specifically to create something new.[14]

My first job in Arizona was at the Four Seasons Resort in Scottsdale. Although I didn't interact with one of my bosses often, he slowly started to teach me what it could be like to have a father figure who appreciated my authenticity. Because of him, I started to feel better about receiving guidance, feedback, and care from an authority figure. It was a breakthrough. He genuinely got to know me by asking many insightful questions. I learned a lot from him about listening, empathy, and the power of questions. He taught me about emotional intelligence, how to handle conflict, and effective communication. While I certainly didn't understand the concept of having a soul group at that time, I deeply appreciated how he invested his time to make sure those around him had the training and mentorship they needed to thrive.

In 2010 I began working in human resources at Banner Health. My boss there helped me dive even deeper into self-discovery and became like a secondary mother. She offered me a new level of understanding around the concept of family that I hadn't considered before. She started to teach me how to influence others at scale. She helped my story get published in Banner's employee newsletter, which was distributed to 27,000 employees. She taught me a scripted leadership process and how to roll out programs to large organizations.

I remember making questionable decisions as a supervisor in my family's business. At Banner, I learned how to lead intentionally and influence others. This was a big transition for me, and I wouldn't have been able to do that without guidance from my soul group. In 2013, I met my stepdaughter, Aleah. I dated her mom for seven years. Aleah has been my biggest catalyst for growth and is the person I credit for starting me down the aligned path I walk today. She teaches me to live experientially, in the moment, and to trust the process of life. I'll share more about her in chapter 5.

As time passed, it became obvious to me there's a connection between beings that doesn't necessarily have to come from blood relation. I met Jessica in August of 2016; we were both members of Valley Leadership's Class 38. When I shook her hand, I had a weird feeling of safety. This kind of thing began to happen to me more and more. I met Patricia in 2010 when we both worked for Banner Health. We reconnected in 2017, and I realized she's another key member of my soul group. Each time these special individuals came into my life, I felt safe and understood. I would feel like I could say anything and trust the other person unequivocally. As more souls entered my life this way, I began to feel I was part of something far bigger than just myself.

Now, I meet new members of my soul group almost monthly. When it happens, I find myself being called to offer my time to that individual in a way that benefits us both.

Debbie, my hairstylist, is another key member of my soul group. We met in 2013, and no matter where I lived, where I was traveling, or how my schedule evolved, I still found a way to be in her chair each month. Stylists make us physically beautiful, listen and hold space, and often serve as counselors offering ideas that provide clarity. In so many ways, Debbie has become a sister to me, offering me acceptance and appreciation no matter what was transpiring in my life.

Who is in your soul group, and how have they helped you?

Growth Through Connection

Humans are a social species. We seem to learn more and ascend more smoothly to our life's next level by sharing our story. And through seeing our story in others. I met an artist named Sara a while back. She had been following me on social media, liking and sharing my content. I appreciated her engagement and comments. Eventually, she reached out to me and we had a wonderful conversation. I knew she would not want to pay my regular fees, but my soul felt called to coach her. I felt that nudge, that knowing: the universe had brought us together for a reason. So, I said, "I want to offer my VIP day to you, Sara. Instead of completing it in one day, let's spread that time together over three Saturdays, and in exchange, I want you to paint a piece that represents my soul."

Sara was one of the most engaged clients I'd ever had. She did tremendous work on herself, considerable emotional shedding, and made new connections for me in terms of the impact I could have on a person. It was a fulfilling experience, working together to unlock her potential and realign her with her Earth school curriculum on those three mornings.

To create my painting, she submitted a questionnaire to me. It asked questions such as "Which artists do you admire and why? What art styles do you connect with most? What symbols and colors are most important to you? How do you want this work of art to make you feel? What message do you want this piece to convey?"

She ended up painting a four-by-six-foot canvas of a lion's face and mane whose fur morphed into feathers. In the background, there was a wavy body of water and a beautiful sun. I found her work to be stunning and incredibly representative of who my soul is. There are myriad reasons why the universe placed Sara in my soul group. Her life's journey with her mother was strikingly similar to my journey with my father. For years, I jumped from job to job, relationship to relationship, and client to client, thinking some new level of fulfillment would greet me on the other side. I was, of course, avoiding my deepest emotions. The universe was trying to teach me: "Michael, you have to get deeper in your emotional journey if you truly desire to ascend to the next level."

Sara had to work through something similar to process loss and release aspects of her mom that were no longer benefitting her. Sara's mom's curriculum was quite different than Sara's. Her mom encouraged her to keep her emotions muted, to work for a reliable and stable employer, and to choose life's safe routes. Me asking Sara to create the painting she did was my purposeful play to encourage her to feel safe in losing the approaches to art that made her comfortable previously. The result of her shedding her old style and experimenting with new ones has allowed Sara to paint murals the size of buildings. The art she creates today is far more diverse than what she painted in 2018. As she has expressed herself more and taken on more entrepreneurial projects, opportunities flow to her steadily. Because she's consciously choosing to dive deeper into her emotions, Sara's projects are now much grander in scale. What I love about this is that the world is seeing just how bold, big, and beautiful Sara's soul is.

Sara named her painting for me *Parallels*. Fitting in so many personal and metaphorical ways. My life's progression isn't that different than Sara's. As I've gone deeper into exploring my emotions, the projects I'm working on are on a different scale as well. Like me, Sara jumped from job to job to job, thinking she was going to discover happiness in the next one. Happiness lay dormant in her the entire time. Once she shed the beliefs her mom instilled in her at a young age, she felt free to do what her inner knowing was nudging her to do.

From Loss to Healing

Humans are hard-wired to feel safe in repeating the same habits daily. When those habits are disrupted, feelings of unknowing, helplessness, dis-ease take hold. If you feel unsure about what to do next . . . that's exactly how you should feel, and that's okay. The Age of Aquarius is a time of tremendous expansion. We're breaking outdated habits. People are recognizing their true power. Earth is healing. And we're being given a green light to create a new society where diversity, uniqueness, and authenticity are honored. One where the previously underserved will be lifted. One where we move from lack to abundance.

Sometimes, when one path is blocked, it's easy to stop trying. We give up. We feel defeat. But if you're determined, adaptable, and open to a bit of magic, immense joy may be waiting for you. To wrap up this chapter and begin moving you from feelings of loss to peace, I want to highlight a few things Cleopatra has taught me. Without her important work here on Earth, this book may not exist. She has taught me:

1. Almost overnight, humans are learning that money, power, and fame mean little. The idea of celebrity and idolizing someone else is leaving with the Age of Pisces. Cleo reminds us that what is inspiring, motivating, and worthy of time is the pet that lies beside us on the couch while we take conference calls.
2. Being loved, valued, and appreciated for who you are comes from the beauty of your soul, being emotionally sensitive to others, and living an aligned life. You don't need makeup, branded clothing, a certain body shape, the partner who looks good on paper, or a house in the

right neighborhood. Cleo hasn't altered her appearance since birth, and I love her deeply for how she walks on a leash, plays fetch, and chases lizards around the backyard. Take a second closer look at those near you and love their souls, not their physical appearance.

3. Being respected is far more valuable than being popular. There will be several versions of you in this lifetime—some socially accepted, some not. Cleo understands that each life phase teaches us important lessons that help us help others and continually earn their trust. When confronted by change, seek to be appreciated, trusted, respected.

Experiencing loss allowed me to understand the process of transformation in a much deeper way than I would have had I not gone through it. The losses I've experienced paved the way to the beautiful present I'm now living. Embedded within the most painful moments in our lives are gifts if we're reflective enough to see them. This part of the *I Know* journey is weighted heavily toward telling, sharing, and releasing your stories, and less weighted toward taking action. All it really requires of us is being willing to walk into our painful moments to begin to let them go.

Key Takeaways

- In the unknowing and uncertainty of life, there is opportunity.
- Anytime we experience change, we will feel a sense of loss.
- We each experience loss differently, and the feeling of loss is valid no matter how big or small it is perceived to be.

- Create psychological safety to make mistakes, try new approaches, and find your life's intended path.
- To fully release the sense of loss, we must be still, go within, and process undealt-with emotions.
- The pace of societal change is increasing and will disrupt healthcare, universities, travel, and much more.
- Dr. Bruce Lipton's research proves that what we learn from birth to age seven subconsciously guides our choices for the remainder of our lives.
- Earth has transitioned from the Age of Pisces into the Age of Aquarius.
- Dr. Martin Seligman's three P's teach us the temporary nature of loss: we're not at fault, a change will not affect every facet of our lives, and we'll not feel the loss for the rest of our lives.
- Each day, think: Less, but better. Less, but better. Less, but better.
- Use the Schumann resonance to your benefit by connecting with Earth physically and lowering your body's electromagnetic activity.
- Every human has their own hero's journey and will experience life's ups and downs—repeatedly.
- Members of your soul family will support you each step of your journey. You are never alone.
- Sara served as a mirror for me, helping me process loss at deeper levels.
- Expect nothing and appreciate everything.

Chapter 2: Fear

When dealing with people, remember you are not dealing with creatures of logic, but with creatures of emotion. ~Dale Carnegie

Once in a while, the stated reason an executive hires me to coach them or consult their business is not the *real* reason.

Let me explain what I mean by sharing a story.

If you needed capital for a mutual fund, Tom could find you millions of dollars *tomorrow*. He had the right connections and instincts to know how to close deals. However, Tom had a challenging childhood. He was born to two parents who had three kids each with their previous spouses. Tom was born, by surprise, as the seventh child. His siblings are far older than he is; some of them are no longer alive.

He was the overlooked child, the person who needed to constantly prove himself. Tom figured out a way to scratch and claw his way to prominence by becoming an excellent golfer. He made a name for himself on mini-tours and is regularly crowned club champion at one of Arizona's most prestigious private clubs. At some point in Tom's journey, he hurt his back and was no longer allowed to progress further in his professional golf career. He transitioned away from golf into financial services and leveraged his relationships to close deals.

To prove his worth, Tom would take risks on deals that didn't work out for one reason or another. Yet he had to project the image of being successful, even when what was happening behind closed doors wasn't helping him accomplish his goals.

On one of his prosperous deals, the way Tom and his clients celebrated was by doing lines of cocaine late into a New York City night. The feeling of accomplishment and glory was so beneficial for Tom that he continued his addiction for the next 18 months. I believe he was trying to connect emotionally again to what he felt in happier times in his life. Unfortunately, Tom was having fewer and fewer professional wins. His deal pipeline was drying up.

That's when he called me and asked if I could improve communication between him and his business partner and help him manage his time more effectively.

I coached them both for a little over three months, and we were making solid progress. My processes were turning the business in a positive direction, and I enjoyed my time with them. Then, early one morning, Tom called me extremely disheveled. He said, "Hey man, I need to tell you the real reason why I hired you."

It was a surreal moment.

I said, "I'm ready, brother."

He said, "I crashed my car into a telephone pole. I overdosed on cocaine. I need you to do two things. I need you to save my business, and I need you to save my marriage."

I agreed to help.

Tom sought medical help and met with his physician to slowly rid himself of the cocaine dependency. He also saw a therapist monthly to explore how what happened in his childhood drove him down the path of relying on the drug. My work transitioned rapidly to assess whether or not Tom's business partner would stay or if we'd have to adjust the business's revenue models. Tom's business partner left. This opened the door for Tom to shed revenue lines that were no longer viable and to recommit to opportunities more closely aligned with his communication style and strengths.

I also had numerous conversations with Tom's wife to explain what I thought was happening. Until the car crash, she was completely unaware of her husband's addiction.

I ultimately did what Tom asked me to do that fateful morning.

To save the marriage, I offered Tom's wife the same behavioral assessment I used to coach Tom and his business partner. Because Tom had absorbed my coaching well, he and I worked through how to tailor his communication to her style so she'd feel heard and accepted. On our every-other-week calls, I let her vent and cry and brought new light to how his life's circumstances led him where they did. Finally, I coached them both on finding new levels of commonality, doing weekly activities to rebuild trust, and more openly sharing their journeys. They have two daughters, both in college at the time. I love that this family was willing to do things they hadn't before and emerged better together from a challenging time.

At the root of what happened in this story was fear—Tom was afraid of not being perceived as accomplished, of not being heard or seen. He did cocaine to continually recreate the feeling of success and acceptance that his parents didn't offer him years ago. The universe interjected in having the crash occur to slow Tom down. He needed to shed what he wished his parents would have done so that new doors could open and allow him to confront his fears and learn to feel loved for being his authentic self. When we're unwilling to confront difficult emotions, we often use numbing behaviors that can be hurtful to ourselves and to our family.

That's what this chapter is about: facing our emotions, our deepest fears, and processing them intentionally so we can let them go and welcome new blessings. When we fail to do this, the consequences can be life-threatening.

The obstacle is the path.
Overcoming a fear gives you strength and elevates you to
your life's next level.

Tom's business has evolved into a marketing and branding platform for investment offices. He is in a considerably better place emotionally. For some reason, I knew—based on what he and his business partner repeatedly talked about—that moving away from leveraging Tom's relationships only in face-to-face meetings was the path forward. Being able to scale the best practices of how Tom established and deepened relationships allowed him to help more people and created a more consistent revenue flow. Although the business partner isn't with him, they're still friends, and Tom is on an aligned path for his skillset, his interests, and where he can add the most value to his clients. Finally facing his past and releasing his fears freed Tom to no longer have to prove himself. He could simply be his authentic self.

Confronting My Fears

Fear has held me back at every stage of life. As a teenager, I did not stand up for my authentic self. I did not attend the honors program at the University of Arizona even though I wanted to. Throughout my 20s, I didn't connect to, understand, and try to support my wife in living her curriculum, so she left me. I attended the Thunderbird School of Global Management, yet never once gave a public presentation in a class. In my early 30s, I stayed in a physically abusive relationship where I was pushed down a flight of stairs. I budgeted poorly, didn't sell myself well to potential clients, and tried to "save" my family without realizing it wasn't my role to do so.

For decades, I've been unwilling to tell my story for fear of being criticized. I stayed in unserving relationships for too long, and I worked for too many clients for free because I feared they wouldn't like me if I charged them my normal fees.

The thing I fear most is having my life's work available at scale, for so many more people to see my life's journey. I worry whether the processes and the ways I've helped others will be received well by new audiences. Can people worldwide benefit from my ideas regardless of their socio-economic status? I fear criticism of my processes and that I'll be hard on myself for not conducting additional research or for releasing the information before society was truly ready for it.

I also fear the loss of control of my time. I irrationally worry my life will change dramatically and the days of being in one place, not traveling, will disappear. But my message—that people know their soul's mission and must be empowered to live it out—is simply too important to shrink away from. The message must be spread and spread widely.

For me, coaching a person one-to-one is something I've done thousands of times. My life's next level includes taking these processes and considering how to integrate them into society. I don't know what that's going to bring; I don't know how these processes will change. And I don't know how people are going to be affected by them. When millions of people look at my work, I won't be able to control what they think or do. But I also know I have to do this to ascend to my next level. I need to challenge myself and pursue this incredibly big and scary dream so I can truly find peace in myself and my journey.

The Algorithm of Your Life

With influences from astrology and numerology, there is a multitude of factors that create your Earth school curriculum. Before birth, I believe your soul agrees to incarnate on Earth and experientially learn specific karmic lessons. The Pattern app, the World Numerology app, and the Co-Star app each help reveal what our curriculum may be. The book *Human Design: The Definitive Book of the Science of Differentiation* by Ra Uru Hu, released in 2011 by HDC Publishing, can also offer insights.

The more I study this, the more I realize it is as if roughly 75% of our life on Earth is predetermined by our soul prior to choosing our parents and our bodies. This is the curriculum. How we choose to learn this curriculum, our free will, is up to us moment to moment. That leaves 25% of our life to be made up as we go. Even though we have an inkling of what our curriculum is, the way we learn to overcome fear, for example, doesn't have to happen on a specific day or at a specific time.

There is variability in the circumstances and how the learning actually occurs.

The way the algorithm seems to work is that if we choose to not process an emotion or learn a lesson when it's introduced to us softly, it will come back to us with more intensity until we address it. Envision an upward spiral. If we don't learn the lesson, it'll come back to us at an upper spiral level with even more emotional turmoil. We are continually introduced to the lesson at increasing levels of challenge until we're willing to confront it and process the underlying emotion.

This can be a difficult process for people to wrap their minds around or consider. There's little in conventional Western education that teaches students to openly express and process their emotions. Or to sit in meditation and explore themes in their life's events. If a circumstance continues to enter your life, the universe may be trying to help you release it. I ask clients to journal regularly so they can identify when they felt certain feelings and what was occurring before the feeling emerged. They can then use the feeling as a marker and notice its trigger. It's likely there is a commonality linked to that individual's early childhood years—an origin event of that feeling.

When I agreed to do business with a person who had more wealth than me, I began noticing a recurring feeling that they were taking advantage of or trying to control me. They would do or say something that made me feel less than. As I honored the feeling, meditated on it, and identified the origin of the feeling, I recognized they were doing nothing wrong. I perceived them as having more power than me, the same way I perceived my dad as wielding too much control when I was young. I recognized the universe was moving me up the spiral and reminding me I needed to release my feelings around wealth and power. When I did so, people in power positions stopped triggering me.

Tom was confronted numerous times prior to crashing his car into the telephone pole. As the universe walked him higher up his spiral, it is as if he needed to crash to make his addiction known to those close to him. It may have been months before he shared it with them. If you're given a sign from the universe about an emotion or behavior, and it comes to you softly three times, take action on it as quickly as possible. Avoid letting it get to the point it's that intense. Life's free will component is such that you get to choose where, on that upward spiral, you process the emotion.

Fearful Predictions

Do you fear change? As I connect the dots between current events, I've come to believe society will experience immense evolution between 2020 and 2030. My intuition guides me to share a handful of transformations I think possible. What's coming? What will our futures hold? What should you prepare for?

- Healthcare: Western nations shift from a pure focus on allopathic medicine and integrate homeopathic techniques to address how emotions create physical illness. Most pharma companies disappear as focus moves from masking symptoms to preventing illness.
- Media: Corruption from money and advertising will be removed as the driving influence over content is replaced by content of character and what best serves all stakeholders.

- Financial systems: A gold-backed quantum financial system will create transparency in transactions. Debt will become illegal and a universal basic income will be given to all. Income tax will be abolished and replaced by a sales tax on non-essential goods.
- Politics: Federal governments will shrink in size and more decision-making control will sit locally. We'll see a rise in grassroots global movements and new nations will form.
- Religion: People will find new meaning in and see religious teachings as metaphors to help pull answers out of themselves.
- Education: Universities will consolidate as in-class rote memorization learning will be replaced by online learning and learning from peers and experiences.
- Upheaval: Another coronavirus, or something similar, will return in 2030, and there will be an additional awakening like the one experienced in 2020. Society may change even more than it did in 2020. After that, viruses will leave humanity.
- Energy: There will be adoption of Nikola Tesla's inventions for free energy and the movement away from fossil fuel usage.
- Oneness of all beings: Outdated patriarchal systems will crumble and be replaced by ways of being where all, including the planet, are respected equally.
- Work: You won't have to work; you'll be given the choice to. You can choose to work on a societal need that's interesting to you or that you're passionate about.

How did you feel reading these ideas? Excited? Fearful? In either case, you have the means to process your feelings and consider the future intentionally.

Will you react to change, or will you create it?

Rules for Life

In 2019, I was invited back to the high school I attended to share with its current students highlights from my professional journey and rules for life. It was such a meaningful experience for me. At the core of my rules for living is authenticity. I believe all persons deserve an opportunity to become the most authentic version of themselves, to understand their Earth school curriculum, and—without being interrupted or stopped—to go through life in whatever way they see fit. Our society says you should attend grade school, head off to college, secure a dependable job, and then retire around a certain age. I genuinely want people to honor that script as being right for some, but they can live life in whatever way they desire as long as it's not harmful to others.

My second rule centers on creating social connectedness. To uncover your most authentic self, the people you surround yourself with are one of the best learning methods. The strongest drug for a human is another human. True learning occurs experientially, and we should be interacting with others to solidify learning. Relationships teach us vulnerability and courage and help us release past traumas and old shame, and to be accepted . . . to advance and to grow to the next stage of our lives. As the noted shame and vulnerability researcher Brené Brown says in her bestselling book *Daring Greatly*, "Because true belonging only happens when we present our authentic, imperfect selves to the world, our sense of belonging can never be greater than our level of self-acceptance."[15]

The third rule is what I've struggled with most: trusting the process. I'm an introvert. My brain thinks linearly. It works well when there's a set process. As much as we want to solve problems overnight, that's often not the path of transformational growth. We're meant to experience a pain-to-purpose journey where problems, challenges, and difficult emotions teach us more than we could learn any other way. I had only experienced soft, on-the-surface emotions for the first 38 years of my life. Then all of a sudden, I was put into a place of significant darkness, where I was forced to dive much deeper into understanding my emotions. I had little choice but to trust the process. I had to trust that the transitions in my business and relationships were ultimately going to be for my long-term benefit.

It turned out that it was.

I'm in a new relationship. Tiffany entered my life and has been a significant blessing. The things I longed for in a partner, she is. Professionally, I've supported an organization as they changed their culture; I could not have done that before. I'm slowing down, remaining patient, doing hard work emotionally, and trusting that what's coming will be ideal for my learning.

Living my rules has involved confronting fear. If you're living life differently than much of society, my guess is a lot of fear is coming up for you as well. One sign your fear is active right now is an emotional outburst. An individual's negative emotion today can often be attributed to not addressing or seeking counseling for a past emotional hardship. According to the Hulnicks' book *Loyalty to Your Soul*, all emotional reactivity today is due to an old unhealed wound.[16] A potential impact of not releasing pent-up emotions is an unexpectedly strong outburst toward your colleagues, clients, or family members.

If you ever find yourself having an out-of-proportion reaction, it is beneficial to change your location as quickly as possible and find someone to talk with. Once in a different, and private, location breathe deeply (inhale, hold, exhale for eight seconds each) to lower your heart rate. For more insight and tips about releasing emotion, please refer to the next chapter.

From there, I have a tried-and-tested process for moving through your fears.

1. Openly acknowledge and accept your fears are real by writing down or verbalizing the following: "I fear ___ because ___." Examples:

- I fear remaking my resume or LinkedIn profile because I'll have to acknowledge my accomplishments and wins.
- I fear traveling to a new place because I might experience discomfort or embarrassment by not knowing the local customs or language.
- I fear sharing strong opinions, on social media or otherwise, because then I'll be visible and accountable to more people when I make mistakes or learn new information.

2. Feel and describe any associated emotions that come up for you when you talk about your fears, such as embarrassment, envy, or anger. It's valuable to explore questions such as "When I think about ___, how do I feel? Why? What is the origin event of this emotion?" to release old, stale emotions. *Talk* about your fear or fears. Find a friend, counselor, mentor, or coach you trust and work through your fears. Look right at them. Get them out of your body. Be curious. By doing so, you'll reduce the power you're giving the fear.

- There are six core human emotions: love, fear, disgust, surprise, anger, and sadness.[17] This has always struck me as being odd . . . that most of them are negative. I've come to understand that Earth is a place where souls choose to experience life and release negative emotions. Often, you have to release one of the negative emotions to gain access to a good one.

3. Approach doing the thing you fear by adopting a learning mindset. Remind yourself that making mistakes is expected and a key component of learning. The goal isn't to get it right or be perfect the first time. Mentally treat it like practice. Simply practice doing the thing you fear, and with each iteration will come new insights. In releasing expectations of yourself, you open yourself to new possibilities your brain hasn't yet considered.

- The Mindful Engagement process developed by the University of Michigan is an understanding that when you walk into doing something you've never done before, the goal is *learning*. By taking a learning mindset, you release all fear of being judged. The process is built on approach, action, and reflection.[18]

4. Take action by repeatedly trying the feared activity. Do each iteration of your action purposefully, completing the activity until you feel increasing comfort performing it.

- It's about repetition: doing the thing you fear consistently. What you think that you can't do will feel less scary when you do it. I've been skydiving three times now. The first time I did it, I was afraid at each step of the process—my body was shaking. Landing the first time, I was so overwhelmed with fear that I just sat there, immobilized on the ground. Each successive time I did it, I felt far less afraid. When I go skydiving again, I'll feel 90% less fear than I did the first time.

5. Reflect on your process of learning without judgment. Give yourself time. As philosopher Jiddu Krishnamurti says, "The ability to observe without evaluating is the highest form of intelligence." Journal or contemplate answers to the following questions:

- What did you feel?
- What went well?
- What didn't go well?
- What will you do differently next time?
- Who will you share this with? When we learn lessons in our lives, the best way to learn them is to teach them with others.
- How has your self-concept changed as a result of the action you took? For example, skydiving built my confidence. It made overcoming other fears easier.

After you've completed these steps, you'll have the experience to not let fear stop you from leading your ideal life. You'll have learned that your fears were based on irrational, untrue emotions. As you confront and overcome fears, help from a trusted friend is often the difference between release and further suffering. Pain is not suffering. Staying stuck in pain is suffering.

The Soul Body

Western societies have been designed to place allopathic medicine and the treatment of the physical body's symptoms first. I don't know how much people think about preventing illness through understanding their soul body.[19] They're not aware of the impact of not processing emotions over long periods—the effect that it has on our soul and on the body's seven chakras, the energy centers of the body. There are people who believe in and practice caring for their soul body, but many don't openly discuss it. Over extended periods, the body has the capacity to turn negative energy into physical sickness. I think of this as a way to alert us that we need to make adjustments to how we're navigating life. I believe the things that happen to us physically unfold as they do to teach our soul some important lesson.

When I interact with clients and realize they are suffering from an illness, I grab Karol Truman's insightful book *Feelings Buried Alive Never Die* and research that sickness.[20] I incorporate what I learn into my coaching. I want to connect the disparate dots in that individual's life, and I know that what happens to them physically is a sign of how they're feeling emotionally. Especially if they're not capable of expressing it to me. Then, I'm able to ask different questions to get them to release the emotion so the illness lessens or disappears and they can move one step closer to realigning with their curriculum.

If a person is going down an unaligned path because they're not processing fear, there are any number of things that may show up in their body physically. Using Truman's book, people can self-diagnose. If they don't know what to look for in their emotional histories, identifying the physical pains they're experiencing can be illuminating. In the last chapter, I mentioned my pull to eating sugar. For as long as I can remember, my body on the BMI scale was borderline obese. Even though I knew better, I defaulted to eating simple carbs because I didn't feel safe. I felt uneasy on the path I was traveling, about a person I was with, or in my decisions. So, to feel secure, I overate to feel full and to prove to myself that I was provided for.

Another example of this concept is my clients who have verbal stutters. According to Truman, it is generally because they were suppressed as children. Any time they attempted to speak up, they were not allowed to. As they attempted to speak against a parent or an authority figure and were punished for doing so, they developed the stutter.

My father was diagnosed with hairy cell leukemia in 1995. According to Truman's research, cancer can be a sign you're unhappy with your path in life or your previous choices. That you wish you would have chosen something different. Of course, you might be or know a person who received a cancer diagnosis at a very young age, and it just felt so random, yet even a cancer diagnosis is there to teach us something important about our soul's journey.

In no way am I saying to stop seeing your physician. I'm helping you to see your body through a new lens and offer yourself new information so you can take more control over your life.

Find Commonality

Uncertainty is a cause of fear, too. There is a lot we don't know. Fortunately, we have the opportunity to treat people around us with different experiences and opinions as resources, not as threats or enemies. As events occur, honor that the person next to you has an opinion potentially opposite to yours. That doesn't make either party right or wrong. It does make for an interesting discussion about what childhood events shaped someone's perspective, patterns of challenging emotional events throughout life, who they admire, or why they believe what they do.

As you share your stories, understand that true learning occurs when the other person has experienced life while in your shoes, has felt your emotions, and was forced to make the choices you did. Everyone's opinion is valid. Their experiences are valid. Their choices are valid. Instead of comparing and looking for differences, find anything you share in common and start there.

This is why I've chosen to share my story with you even though I feel afraid to do so. My hope is you'll find at least one thing we have in common, and from there, we can both grow.

As I work to release my fears and embrace uncertainty by learning more from the people around me, I like to keep this quote from Japanese writer Haruki Murakami in mind: "Always remember that to argue, and win, is to break down the reality of the person you are arguing against. It is painful to lose your reality, so be kind, even if you are right."

Key Takeaways

- It's time to believe in yourself and others.
- Offer everyone the benefit of the doubt. We're all doing the best we can.
- Being divided into "us" versus "them" groups does not help humanity rise.
- By confronting fears, we no longer have to prove ourselves. We can simply be authentic.
- Silence is more powerful than attempting to prove your point.

- If you avoid addressing a fear, it will return with increasing intensity until you choose to process it. You may take action that is more hurtful than helpful.
- When you choose to not confront your fears, negative energies remain in your body, blocking your chakras. These blocks are likely to cause physical illness.
- When the universe offers you soft signs to confront a fear, do so as quickly as possible.
- Between 2020 and 2030, Earth will experience tremendous change.
- The strongest drug for a human is another human.
- Words don't teach. Experiences do.
- If you, or others near you, are having emotional outbursts, that's a sign fear is being confronted.
- All fears must be openly acknowledged to be fully released.
- All experiences, opinions, and choices are valid. Instead of focusing on differences, we can uplift one another by finding what we have in common.
- How you are feeling physically offers insights into how well you're releasing emotions.

Chapter 3:
Emotional Release

Most persons are so absorbed in the contemplation of the outside world that they are wholly oblivious to what is passing on within themselves. ~Nikola Tesla

Michael at Age 6

There were many circumstances from my younger years I've reckoned with recently. I wish to share them with you. As Brené Brown so wisely says, shame and trauma decrease when we talk about them. Sharing our stories is a powerful way to begin to process and release our emotions, which is the focus of this chapter.

I want to preface this section by saying these are *my* memories, *my* journey, *my* learning. How others felt during these years and how they remember them may be different and is equally valid. Also, I recognize each of us navigates life with different traumas. There are different levels of privilege in coping with these events. The magnitude of traumas fluctuates, but the process and effort used to release the emotions may be similar. I feel there is value in sharing my journey in the hopes that it unlocks doors for others.

In March 1980, I was born jaundiced and raised in a house built in the late 1800s that my grandparents owned. For most of my childhood, it had a wood furnace in the basement for heat, no central air conditioning, and was surrounded by fields. As a child, I experienced isolation, both literally and emotionally. Snowstorms stranded us in our home. My sister Amy and I were expected to work from a young age splitting wood, doing yard work, and, as we came of age, working full time for the family business. We were offered limited time with friends.

In our small town, Christian theology was the norm. It was highly patriarchal. Alcohol was most people's means of escape. I didn't understand my spirituality or emotional intelligence until much later in life. There were very limited choices in meals, TV shows, and fun things to fill time. I didn't like eating meat. I watched bigger farms treat their animals poorly and promised myself I wouldn't contribute to the suffering. I'm a vegetarian and learned in 2017 I have a genetic marker for preferring a plant-based diet.

My family spent most of our time with our closest neighbors and cousins. Diversity in thought, perspective, or experience wasn't the norm. Whatever Christmas gifts my cousins received, my sister and I received. Family competition and jealousy were stifling. We didn't interact with different races, religions, or intellects. We interacted with homogeneity.

I was quiet, shy, a perfectionist, introverted, and rule-following by nature. I avoided conflict.

When I was with an energy healer in 2018, she was very clear about the need for me to examine circumstances that occurred when I was six years old. I sat in meditation quite a bit over the last couple of years to understand what was going on in my family at that time. My sister was four. My mom, Robin, and my dad seemed really unhappy in their relationship and consistently accused the other of being unfaithful. Each parent would come to my sister and me and ask us questions about what the other was doing.

We were too young to know, so we did our best to keep any semblance of peace. I'll never forget those days in different places around the house trying to find feelings of safety. Living on an isolated farm, we had nowhere to escape. Yet they would continually ask Amy and me what the other parent was saying or doing. That put me in a place of constant fear: "What is Dad going to ask me next when I wake up tomorrow? What is it that I'm going to be pressured to tell mom about Dad?"

I started to feel emotionally abandoned. Who was I supposed to trust? Amy was too young to be able to understand what was going on. Clearly, I was too. My mom was more evolved and balanced emotionally, but my dad made most of the money so he seemed to get his way more often. I was beyond confused about what I was allowed to say and what I was not allowed to say and who was right. Because they were both accusing the other, I didn't have a stable guiding light—a parent that served a feeling of stability. So I became entrenched in going quiet, being quiet, and not doing anything that would ruffle feathers. I found myself avoiding both of them so I didn't have to see or hear what was going on.

I'm not unique in this sort of experience, by the way. Most humans have adverse childhood experiences, shortened to the acronym ACEs by researchers at the University of Tennessee.[21] I scored a 4 out of 10 on the quiz when in 2017 I stumbled across an article explaining it and decided to answer the questions. As we discussed in the last chapter, the basis of physical illness may be unaddressed or unexpressed emotions—and each of us has them.

It felt more isolating as time passed. I felt more and more alone because I didn't want to be the tattletale. I didn't want to say anything. The less information I had, the better off I was. Unfortunately, my close relationship with Amy faltered when I became a teenager. The lawn maintenance business started to do better financially then, and I was allowed to buy a brand-new car on my 16th birthday. My head got big and I began emulating my father's behavior.

To feel accepted by my dad, I started treating my sister poorly. My dad would make jokes about her or my mom's appearance. I echoed his behavior because he offered me what I thought I wanted, which was rounds of golf and the car and power to supervise teams inside the family business. Of course, unbeknownst to me at the time, I was doing things that were significantly hurtful to my mom and to my sister. After moving to Arizona, my communication with Amy became limited. We do have an open, loving, and caring relationship today, but that came from investing in her and her family, learning more about her curriculum, and asking for her forgiveness.

My gut tells me Amy is still finding peace with my parent's behavior from back then. About five years ago, I started to really look at the mistakes I made and what my teenage years were like for those close to me. I was clear with Amy that I was deeply sorry for what I said and did during that time. I hope she heard me, but it is okay if she didn't. For the rest of my life, I will work to right old wrongs with her. I envy her soul's strength being the second child born after an emotionally unintelligent older brother. Though I do believe all souls choose their Earth school curriculum, feeling the emotion of who I was is still hard for me.

I continually own my mistakes and am consistent in reaching out to her and her kids, not to make up for the past, but to help us both heal over extended periods of time. I also genuinely want to be a part of my niece's and nephew's lives. There's so much I can learn from them.

Generational Curses

Over the last two years, I thought more deeply about my parent's curriculum. Why did they fight? What did their parents teach them? Which parent did they struggle to connect with when they were young? My grandfather Herb built the family business and then passed away in 2002. He was born at a time in human history, in the 1930s, where you were a *worker*. Cradle-to-grave employment was the way of life, and he only had one employer his entire life. He worked first shift for decades and grew his business nights and weekends from 1953 until 1987 when he passed it to my father.

My father and his three younger sisters learned that for six days each week, they would rarely see Herb. Sunday was church and family day. My dad and his three sisters were "encouraged"—the same way that my cousins, Amy, and I were—to work for the business. If I wanted to play basketball with friends or if I wanted to compete in a golf tournament, I was told "no" more often than not because I needed to work.

I think people from Herb's generation believed if you work, you create safety.[22] If you work, you create stature in the community. If you work, you have a brand. That belief pattern was passed to my father, and in the 90s and early 2000s, he was able to make the business even bigger and more successful than it had been.

In the late 1980s, my dad bought a pickup truck and put a sticker on the dashboard that said, "The road to success is uphill. Unless your father owns the business." My father seemed to need to prove Herb wrong—prove he was his own authentic self—by not being dictatorial or authoritarian.

Yet even when he tried to be empathetic and collaborative, he still came across as authoritarian. He didn't know any better. In the early part of my growth and especially in moving to Arizona, I tried hard to prove myself. I didn't want to be known as Jack Seaver's son. Yet I can work tirelessly for extended periods of time and labor 70 hours a week because that's the way I was raised. I am Jack Seaver's son.

To break my family's generational curse of following in our fathers' footsteps, I had to release my desire to be better than my father or grandfather. I had to accept how their influence shaped and helped make me who I am. I think I've done this. I have separated from my family's belief patterns, ways of living, income, emotional responses, and more. I've introduced and found success living the idea that each of us should be able to travel our own paths, in our own time.

Our families do teach us about love, but we do get to redefine that for ourselves. I was taught that love is earned, that my value was in how hard I worked, and that esteem is built through financial achievement.

I've come to reject those ideas. But I'm not rejecting my family. I love them more than ever.

There's been this nagging belief in the back of my mind that, for my soul to come full circle, to continue the family legacy, and to be closer to my sister and her family, I will need to return, for a few months each year, to Michigan in 15 to 20 years' time.

From a Need to Control to a Willingness to Release

I look back at those years in Michigan and realize I missed the time with my friends. My childhood was focused on work. I lacked a connection with people. There were limitations placed on my most memorable experiences.

In my 20s, I became even more disconnected. I began to realize I was more emotionally limited than I thought previously. It showed up in the way I loved my ex-wife, Kasen. I was always physically there but never emotionally *available* to her. Kasen and I met our sophomore year at Grand Valley State University. We were placed on the same team to complete a class project. Without realizing it, we lived in the same apartment complex, in the same building, on the same floor. Being introverts, we found refuge in doing homework together. We both wished for more independence from our families. We both valued education. We valued quiet.

After she exited a relationship, we began dating and I finally felt like someone understood me. I felt safe. As if I had a kindred spirit. While living in separate small towns in Michigan, we had so many experiences, emotions, and hopes in common. When we moved to Arizona in late 2003, our souls began to separate. As we discovered more of our authentic selves, we came to realize that we no longer needed one another the way we did in college. Through the things we were learning about ourselves, we found new friends who were more closely aligned with who we desired to become. Our work schedules were so different, we rarely had time for one another. I played a lot of golf. She stayed home and read. Besides the gym, we didn't have hobbies we chose to do together. Our souls seemed to be going through rapid ascensions . . . away from the other.

When she decided to end the relationship, I was devastated. She did the right thing, and I'm grateful her choice triggered an awakening in me that wouldn't have happened had she stayed. She taught me to always put my emotions first. To be emotionally available to those near me. To be genuinely interested in another's journey and curriculum and to help them learn it. That controlling how your life looks to others is counterproductive and inauthentic. That the universe will use any means necessary to teach us lessons and help us align with our curriculum. Instead of forcing things . . . I get in flow and trust that what is coming is better suited for my learning than what left.

Kasen was always emotionally developed, and I admired her immensely. The stories she tells on social media now about her husband and his kids show the depth of an amazing soul. When we were together, I was not even remotely close to her level of emotional intelligence. I often think I was unavailable to her because I emulated what I watched my parents do to one another when I was a kid.

In the wake of my divorce, I entered into a series of multiyear monogamous relationships. Reflecting on each, a commonality was that I was still blindly focused on my career as a means of feeling acceptance and love. I hadn't worked through other generational curses yet, so each relationship was loving but only at surface level. I hadn't released what I needed to. I wasn't able to truly connect with each partner.

Starting in late 2017, with the help of an energy healer, I started the journey down to the deep level I exist today. As a result, the relationship I share with Tiffany is full of love, acceptance, and vulnerability. Our relationship resides at a deeper level because of the emotional releasing I did in 2018 and 2019. I needed to experience that pain alone and shed the parts of myself that might not allow me to live authentically or to truly see the beauty of Tiffany's soul and curriculum.

Why Do We Have to Release Our Old Emotions?

Karol Truman's *Feelings Buried Alive Never Die* taught me that if emotions are bottled up, physical illness will occur. We discussed this in the last chapter, but I believe it bears repeating. If we stray further from our life's curriculum, the upward spiral ensures we will continually be confronted by the emotion until it is felt, processed, and released. Until it is, we will endure lost productivity, unhappiness in life, poor relationships, and missed opportunities. Even worse, until we learn to release our old emotions, we will continue to seek comfort in others' answers.

As human beings, we must experience all emotions. The purpose of your Earth walk is to build emotional resilience: to not be triggered by circumstances that used to trigger you.

Steps for Emotional Release

Here are steps you can employ when you feel triggered by a strong emotion.

1. Pause and deeply reflect. When a challenge or stressful situation arises, go for a walk, practice a deep breathing technique, or make time for reflection. If you are able, take 15 to 30 minutes away from people.

To find clarity and identify the right next steps, dive deep into your distant past. What was happening to you and in your world from birth until age seven? How do you unknowingly repeat those same patterns today? As I mentioned earlier, Bruce Lipton's research explains that from birth to age seven, an individual's brain is in the theta brainwave state; after age seven, we move into the beta brainwave state. So the environment around us in the first seven years of our lives is baked into our subconscious.

We unknowingly repeat the habits learned in the theta brainwave state we all experienced from birth to approximately age seven—every day for the rest of our lives, even if they don't benefit us. I recommend investing time to thoroughly understand this period of your childhood. Make notes about what was happening in your home, society, community, school, or wherever you spent time. Then, make a list of the things you're still doing or thinking today that are nearly identical actions or attitudes you watched around you during those early years.

2. Shed old ways of thinking and reacting. Commit to 90 days of weekly practice of thinking or journaling about the habits from your early years that are not helping you accomplish what's coming. Review your notes from step one often. Acknowledge and get curious about:

- Where did it come from?
- What did it teach me?

- How is repeating this holding me back?
- Who can help guide me?
- How do I let it go?

3. Think about what you can do in the current situation and what you'll invite in going forward. Consider what is actually within your control and ask, "What action can I take that is in alignment with my life's purpose?" Then let go of anything that is out of your control. I don't mean change everything all at once. Instead, this step is about small, regular, and manageable changes. If you start your workday at 6:00 a.m., for example, and you'd prefer to start at 9:00 a.m., begin by making the change one day each week. You can increase from there if it feels safe.

During this time of discovery, it's about testing and trying small things that are in alignment with your purpose . . . in a way that's not scary. Try to do this without triggering anxiety or frustration. You're simply experimenting and collecting data on it as you experience it.

4. Finally, put things in perspective and alignment. Remind yourself that whatever is triggering you emotionally right now is a small event on a likely 100-year journey. Try not to assign too much emotional value to it. Simply observe the event and look for the pattern. If a particular thing has happened before, then it's important for you to perhaps ask, "What is the universe trying to teach me? What am I supposed to be learning here?"

Acknowledge and move deeper into the specific actions from the previous step that gave you energy, that gave you a sense of hopefulness, that felt like they were in alignment with what you value. Start to make them part of your normal routine.

Trust the process. Although we can't predict what will happen next, moving into a mental space of believing we can create the lives we want is powerful. The universe will give you opportunities, experiences, and creative outlets to release the old and welcome the new. It will not happen overnight. Even the little things that seem inconsequential can be quite powerful. As time passes, your emotional resilience will increase naturally.

In his book *Zero Limits*, author Joe Vitale tells a story of a psychologist in Hawaii, Dr. Hew Len, who agreed to work at a mental ward in a hospital under the condition that he would not see any of the psych patients in person. As Dr. Hew Len was conducting his work, after three years, the ward was completely empty. But he had never met with any of the patients directly. It is a really interesting story because it shows how we are connected energetically in ways the human eye can't see. Of Earth's electromagnetic spectrum, the human eye can only see .0035% of it. This means you can't see 99.99% of what's actually in front of your face.[23]

What the doctor was able to do was to communicate through thought, ethereally, with each patient to help them release their emotional traumas. Reading Vitale's book taught me that not all accomplishment is physical. The emotional release is just as, if not more, important.

Let Go

We are all connected energetically—in ways our eyes can't see. Each person that comes into our lives teaches us important lessons. I believe we should honor them as they do so.

Shefali Tsabary is a coach for parents who teaches flipping the script with children—to not be authoritarian, or even "parental" necessarily, to their children.[24] Shefali teaches people how to *learn* from their children. She crashes together Eastern methodologies of thought and the interconnectivity of all beings, and suggests that the parents' soul invited that specific child into their life to teach the parent curriculum lessons. Learning more about her work was striking because I had only ever experienced my parents' parenting style. I had limited exposure to other non-Western parenting approaches.

I mention parenting here because I want future generations to have less hardship to overcome in their parent-to-child relationships. The more of Shefali's ideas I absorbed, the more I parented Aleah differently than I had been parented. My parents seemed to want to compete against their friends or siblings for who could give their kids the most: the most things, the most expensive experiences or gifts . . . something they could brag to others about. It was like my parents were trying to make Amy and I idealized versions of what they didn't achieve . . . or become. Their parenting seemed to be more about how they *looked* as parents than the actual impact on the content of Amy and my characters or our emotional well-being.

I wanted to be different. So, instead of forcing Aleah to finish her undergraduate degree at a university, I learned I'd honor her soul more deeply by encouraging her to attend a specialized school closely aligned with her gifts. I learned that her getting a specific job meant far less than her doing work that impacted the community she came to Earth to serve. I learned it was not in Aleah's best interest to emulate my path in life as that would lead to unhappiness for us both. I learned my work with her was to ask questions, offer options, talk through consequences . . . and let her choose knowing I'd love her unconditionally no matter what path she explored.

My relationship with her is much more open than it might have been otherwise. In my behavior toward her, I had watched myself emulate my parents' behavior toward me. When I broke that mindset and began seeing her curriculum for what it is, I started to let go of my past and honor her growth through her journey in her *own* time, in her *own* way.

When my sister and I were young, my dad worked long hours and was in a constant state of stress. And my mom, trying to help him through his anxiety, wasn't always emotionally available. My sister and I did not receive the love we desired, and we've had to release these emotions.

My upbringing had unintended later consequences. For much of my life, I mismanaged money. I bought expensive cars, took trips, and made poor investments. I wasn't taught how to budget, not by my family or the education system. I learned through tough consequences and releasing feelings of what I wished I would've been taught. I had to proactively walk into my own truth by taking online courses, opening new checking and savings accounts, and thinking differently about my relationship with and the purpose of money. I stopped idolizing celebrities and athletes when I realized how money was corrupting them. The infidelity, illegal/unethical business deals, and constant glorification of the wealthy lifestyle at the cost of one's most important relationships, one's own core values, and how far from their Earth school curriculum it took them no longer appealed to me.

As I released the need to be compared to these individuals, I slowly learned to find joy in the moments that had nothing to do with the attainment of wealth. I realized the constant pursuit of money and appearing to be successful was what took my dad's business down in 2008. I released the belief that money was the end . . . and realized that the experiences along the way were the end. Money was simply a tool to create freedom for where I distributed time. Instead of accumulating money, I realized how the accumulation of unique experiences was more important to me than "appearing" successful. I stopped caring what others thought and started caring about how I felt moment to moment. When you treat each experience as though you may never have another like it . . . you live in the moment and enjoy it with all five senses. In chasing money, I wasn't using any of the senses.

Now my parents are in a better place. They're tremendous grandparents. Instead of buying the same gift for each grandchild, they customize the gift to the child's interests. My dad takes my nephew golfing. My mom "buys" the art my niece creates. They've slowed down and enjoy the littlest moments with them. They attend all of their sporting events. At some point in their lives, they made the transition to be parents to their grandchildren in the way they could have been parents to their children.

Transition to the Next Phase of Your Life

My soul chose a curriculum that felt front-loaded with heavy, recurring challenges. The spirit of lions and what they represent are meaningful to me, which is why the painting Sara created was such a blessing to receive. Lions represent perseverance and rising to new heights after being challenged. They represent the courage to overcome challenges. Influencing others positively. They represent a commanding presence. The ability to create your own destiny. Protecting the defenseless. They represent so many things that motivate me and that I appreciate and incorporate into my life.

I've come to accept that in my younger years, I had a rougher go at life than some. I needed to experience this to build emotional resilience to know how to uplift others who experienced hardship. Each morning, I sit in meditation and ask the universe to lift society. Meditation helps me integrate messages from my dreams; helps me keep my body's resonance low on days I knew would be stressful; helps me build confidence through "I am" statements; helps me process and learn from difficult moments; helps me be okay letting go of the need to control someone's perception of me; allows me to visualize and walk through scenarios and possible outcomes; and helps me feel okay with expressing my emotions when I used to keep them bottled up. During this time, I'm not asking for material things for myself: I'm asking to help humanity awaken to the Age of Aquarius in the most beneficial way possible.

Share Your Wins

Nick was the COO of a consulting firm I supported. When he was young, for example, his mother preferred he simply take directions from her and do as she said. When he tried to stand out or do things his way, when he pushed back against her rules, she chased him around their home with an ax. From a young age, he was physically threatened and subconsciously taught to stay behind the scenes.

As Nick moved through his life, he was continually placed on the back burner and told in different ways not to share his story or lead from an authentic place. More than 450 employees reported to him. In our conversations, I quickly saw why he was unwilling to be vulnerable or to discuss his accomplishments with the entire team. In performance reviews, he was told he over-focused on investing time into his favorite employees, going above and beyond for them. But he didn't do it for others.

He played it safe joining well-known boards but got stuck doing the most time-consuming work. Nick did things in a way that would invite the least criticism, not the way that would garner the most involvement and praise from his peers or team.

We worked hard to release the past and create a psychological safety so that he could share his wins with his team. We held a meeting with five of his employees and asked them to give Nick feedback in the meeting . . . but also in the moment (as time passed) to help him see what was and was not working; over three months, I repeatedly texted and asked employees across the firm to over-celebrate his wins to Nick's face and in team meetings.

I attended Nick's team meetings and offered him feedback directly after the meeting; as time went on, he was able to see that his wins would not result in someone chasing him with an ax . . . we could celebrate him for him and that impact he was having on those close to him. He was able to see that his expertise was exactly what his employees needed for succession planning. He realized just how much he loved coaching others and that celebrating his wins taught his employees that it was okay for them to celebrate too. He relished in knowing that his life's experiences had purpose and that they could be used to guide his team to carry on his legacy long after he retired.

The team loved Nick, and sharing wins was the exact thing they needed to see to feel safe to share their own. Their firm did not celebrate personal or division wins nearly enough. One of my tasks was to help implement structures and meeting processes for doing so. They were *forced* to openly share wins, and, consequently, we watched employee engagement scores rise, turnover drop, and revenue increase. This simple habit builds morale. Yet, it's taken many hours of work on my and Nick's part to make this shift.

What's Holding You Back?

The more conversations I have, the more I realize how people have three anchors that hold them back from uncovering their version of authentic happiness. Before you move to the next section of the book, which is all about finding patterns in your life and experimenting with new ways of doing things, it's important to fully acknowledge and process your feelings of loss and of fear around these three main topics:

1. Other people
2. Money
3. Your own past

When someone sees these three things for what they truly are, the faster they release dis-ease, envy, grief, and more. Their lives become simpler, freer, and full of the spiritual, emotional, and material blessings they've desired.

Are you meditating more? The Piscean Age giving way to the Aquarian Age is teaching us that physical and societal achievement is less important than getting into flow with your life's curriculum and receiving the blessings on their way to you.

You can feel safe to invest time into those friends who gift you energy, unlock parts of you that lay dormant, and help you walk toward more aligned experiences. Learning, or crashing together disparate topics, occurs best through experiences with others. Who are you investing in? Your life's journey is meant to be shared. The planet has 7.8 billion talented and authentic souls. We can learn so much from one another if we slow down enough to hear others' stories, what shaped them into who they are, and why they believe what they do.

Love yourself, and those close to you, as much as you secretly want to be loved (if not more).

When you do this, your greatness slowly bubbles to the surface and into your daily thought patterns, beliefs, and behavior. New doors open. Higher heights are reached. You accomplish extraordinary things.

Key Takeaways

- What are you holding onto? Release the old. Welcome the new.

- To rise to higher levels of consciousness, we must shed no-longer-needed parts of ourselves.
- Sharing your personal story is a powerful way to release no-longer-needed emotions.
- You deserve deep fulfillment, happiness, and luck. You may find it by engaging in activity, but you'll more likely find it in stillness.
- Adverse childhood experiences shape our worldview and become an unintentional influence on our daily behavior.
- Each generation passes its ways of being to its children. It is up to the children if they will continue with those beliefs and behavioral patterns or if they will break the generational curse.
- Throughout life, we unknowingly repeat habits we learned from birth to age seven, even if the habits are detrimental.
- Emotional release will not happen overnight. It will take months. Trust the process.
- The human eye can only see .0035% of Earth's electromagnetic spectrum.
- Humans are connected to one another in ways their eyes can't see and their minds can't yet comprehend.
- The most meaningful accomplishments are not physical. They are the emotional release of your adverse childhood experiences and their hold on your subconscious beliefs.
- All persons enter our lives to teach us important lessons.
- Children are your life's greatest teacher. Instead of trying to shape the child into the idealized version of what you weren't able to become, allow the child to be.
- As a parent, are you emulating one of your parent's styles?

- Share your wins openly so others feel safe to share theirs.
- Remember the wise words of Tupac Shakur as you let go of things or people in your life that aren't serving you: "Just because you lost me as a friend doesn't mean you gained me as an enemy. I'm bigger than that, I still wanna see you eat, just not at my table."

Part Two

Discovery

Move through the emotional neutral zone where you'll uncover your core values and personal mission, and set goals to align your time.

Description: *neutral, identity shift*

Actions You're Taking: *stopping the consumption of what hurts me, letting go of the need to control outcomes, using my time more wisely, identifying and owning my emotions, honoring that everyone is doing their best, verifying information before sharing, searching for opportunities*

Challenges You're Encountering: *feeling confusion and ambiguity, low morale and productivity, resentment toward change*

Your Focus: *on me, as in "how am I going to get through this?"*

Ask Yourself: *What new habits can I form? What are my personal core values? How should I change my environment? How often should I communicate? What are my short-term goals?*

To Find Balance, You'll Be Influenced By: *reassurance, clarity, having a plan*

What You Can Communicate to Uplift Others: *express empathy and understanding, outwardly show support, offer frequent updates, share next steps and plans, use metaphors to explain*

Chapter 4: Your Life's Mission

All change is hard at first, messy in the middle, and so gorgeous in the end. ~Robin Sharma

Among the people I've served, a handful of memorable people stand out for the inner wisdom and courage they displayed as we worked together—moving past loss and fear to fully embrace their curriculum and life's purpose.

One of these individuals is a remarkable woman named Avni.

To begin this important section of the book, I'd like to share more of her story with you. In 2019, Avni agreed to a one-day VIP coaching engagement with me. This consisted of a one-hour phone call prior to the VIP day, the day itself, a one-hour phone call 30 days later, and a one-hour phone call 60 days later.

I was impressed by her from the moment we began our work together. As soon as I granted her access to the shared document where I confidentially hosted my questions, processes, and resources for her, she completed the homework and asked many thoughtful questions of me. She read material rapidly, she pulled out insights few others noticed. I was awed by her eagerness and dedication to the process. Avni never worked with a therapist or a coach before. But when we began, she was ready to deeply confront her past and design an aligned future.

She'd not told anyone besides her parents, not even her husband, but Avni had been sexually molested by a family member when she was a small child. After the childhood abuse, she intentionally covered herself, both literally and figuratively—not wanting to be seen, not wanting to share anything about herself. When Avni started college, her first romantic relationship didn't work out because she was unwilling to share anything of herself, fearing that what occurred to her all those years ago would happen again.

Avni was terrified of vulnerability. Although she lacked role models in her younger years, she longed to be the guiding light for those that might be feeling like she did all those years ago. She had loved music at one point in her life but had walked away from it for years. She had also let her love of wellness fall to the wayside. As she put it, "Michael and I met during one of the most difficult periods in my life, both personally and professionally. I was in the middle of a career transition and had a loss in the family. I felt disconnected with everything and wanted to gain control over my emotions and life."

To help her do this, I shared stories from other female leaders who had experienced similar circumstances. I wanted Avni to know that she was not alone, that many others before her had to face their fears and share their truths to move to a better place emotionally. We used a Target Training International Success Insights (TTISI) assessment[25] and a Q&A (which I'll share with you in this chapter) to help Avni see important life patterns. Together, we wrote an authentic mission statement that helped her feel deeply connected to her soul. This proved to be the catalyst to her having more honest communication in her relationships.

In the course of working together, we discovered that Avni's true life's mission was about desiring and having deep emotional connections. The recurring challenge she had in her childhood and throughout her 20s was that she desired deep emotional connections but couldn't open up to be truly intimate with others. She openly recognized her pattern of running from other people, opportunities, her own power, and using her voice. Avni decided she wanted to figure out a way to be a role model. She set a goal to disempower patriarchal power structures while growing women's empowerment.

Identifying an individual's core values is a key component of what I do. You'll learn more about how I examine core values and how they help drive aligned choices later on in this chapter. Once we know the person's life's mission and core values, it's easier to identify what actions will help us realign with our curriculum.

One way that Avni lived her core values was learning. Prior to my meeting with her, Avni had earned two master's degrees and multiple certifications. She's an avid book reader and listens to podcasts. Avni's second core value is power, and until a few months after she and I started working together, she was in a consultative role and had considerable control over her time. She could travel and invest time in her family. Avni started to display her power in new ways, speaking publicly for women in tech groups and for organizations, teaching high school girls and college-age women how to find their paths in tech. She spent more time posting meaningful articles and ideas on LinkedIn. It's been fun to watch her display power in that way.

Another one of Avni's values is compassion. It's been heart-warming to watch her release her frustration toward her family, parent her son differently, and volunteer for a nonprofit. I've seen her move from being closed off and not wanting to express herself or help other people to being able to fully release emotion, spend solid time with her parents in India, and be actively engaged in her son's life.

When she accepted a new role with a financial services organization fully aligned with her life's mission, it was a tremendous win. Her salary increased as she was able to negotiate from a position of strength. She was clear on who she was and what she wanted. She turned down other offers in order to take the one she did—not only for more money, but also for a role that was highly connected to what she desired to accomplish. Avni also joined the board of a global professional women's network dedicated to the professional and economic engagement of women worldwide. She is clearly living from a place of deep purpose and engagement with life.

The last core value of Avni's is the idea of belonging. She is saving to put one of her cousins through school in India. She's chosen to not ignore her family there but rather consciously accept them for what they are even though some members of the family were hurtful to her years ago. Avni is literally investing in the family, proving that belonging remains strong through the good and the bad.

Again, to watch her go from a place of feeling lost and not wanting to express herself to a place where she's got a better relationship with her family—even spending more time with the members of the family that were hurtful to her. That shows she's released old, stale emotions and has welcomed new emotions more closely aligned with her Earth school curriculum.

Her advice for others in a similar place of reckoning in their lives is clear: "Don't expect overnight success. It's a long but transformational process." You'll experience this process yourself as you take action on the steps I've included throughout this book.

I chose to share Avni's story with you because I want you to understand what is possible when you move on from loss and fear, through emotional release, and to a new zone of self-discovery. You are ready to let the old things go and start to explore what is possible in your life. It's exciting, but it's certainly not easy or fast. I'd like to see you approach this part of the journey with curiosity and openness.

Get to know yourself—not the self you've been *told* that you are, but the self that you *really* are.

From a Me to a We Society

In part one, we discussed how our planet has moved into the Age of Aquarius. We are living through considerable change. As the Hulnicks write, when you operate from your soul, not your ego, you'll begin to focus on collective betterment and new doors will open for you.[26] This is what the process of self-discovery promises.

Instead of approaching your job or your relationships from a place of doing what will most benefit you (Piscean Age), it is possible to operate from a place that will help *everyone* concurrently (Aquarian Age). Embracing this idea is a powerful way to get in the flow of change instead of resisting it. Everything that enters your life is a mirror.[27] Other people and circumstances remind us what we are supposed to learn until we actually learn it, and this can take time.

For example, consider our tendency to judge others. Perhaps you felt judged as a child—compared by your parents to a sibling or cousin they considered to be ideal in some way. Because being judged was modeled to you, you subconsciously picked up the habit. Today, you judge others repeatedly, even choosing to tune into reality shows where assessing or ridiculing people for superficial reasons is the entire premise of the show. You are subconsciously, constantly creating an atmosphere of judgment in your life. This will continue until you notice the pattern and choose to stop it, perhaps by getting curious about others and their choices instead of defaulting to judging them simply because they're different than you.

The mirror will then shift. It's not easy work, but it's why we are on Earth. When you begin to deeply understand this, you will not get mad at another person again. It's very freeing.

We are, as they say, all in this together.

In this chapter, I'll present several tools to help you discover your authentic self, find clarity about your curriculum, and write guiding statements to keep you aligned. From there, I invite you to use your clarity for the betterment of others. You may have noticed that the first part of this book was filled with stories and a lot of emotion. This second part will strike a different tone as we move into more objective reflection, experimentation, and pattern-finding.

Humans are happiest when they're learning—overcoming challenges—and helping others overcome a similar challenge for themselves.
To do so, tap into emotions, experiences, and perspectives you may not have had before. Trust the process.

Discovery Tools

During the discovery process, I give my clients the DISC assessment. DISC is an acronym for dominance, influence, steadiness, and compliance and is one of the world's most recognized behavioral assessments. TTISI has certified me to administer their suite of products, the DISC being one of them. These tools are highly credible, based on tested and validated neuroscience.[28] They can offer you a data-driven approach to seeing yourself in an unemotional, objective light, providing a fresh lens through which you can evaluate your choices, both personally and professionally. They can help you better align your time with your Earth school curriculum.

To me, validated assessments tell a person how they'll interact with the world. This self-knowledge can help you better navigate challenges and opportunities. They are also powerful when it comes to knowing what to say yes or no to on a daily basis. By offering objective, third-party research-backed methods, they can help you to communicate clearly and see others without judgment.

DISC Assessment: 1 of 5

Using the DISC assessment in particular, my clients begin to notice patterns in their own observable behavior, tendencies, and habits. This helps them learn how to respond respectfully to others, find win-win resolutions to challenges, and accomplish goals more rapidly. We will explore this first. Because of its validity—we've got 30 years of data to prove that the DISC is accurate—it's a terrific tool.[29]

There are a number of components and key takeaways of a DISC report I focus on during a coaching session. Are you an introvert or an extrovert, task-oriented or people-oriented? Do you see yourself as more or less powerful than the world around you? Do you view the environment around you favorably (you're optimistic) or unfavorably (you're pessimistic)? What do you fear? When stressed, what is your default emotional response? When in conflict or negotiating, what is your preferred style? The pages that follow provide the answers to these questions for each D, I, S, and C type. Knowing these answers about yourself is beyond empowering as it allows you to regulate your behavior. Soon, you'll notice patterns in others' behavior and you'll be able to honor their journey too.

Have you completed a DISC assessment? If so, block time on your calendar to review your report and compare your style to my notes. Perhaps, you'll garner new insights about yourself. If you've not taken the DISC online, consider doing so soon. You may also find value in thinking about people you struggle to communicate with. Based on your awareness of them, what is their DISC profile? How might you use the information below to tailor your communication to them to build trust and deepen the relationship?

Here are my interpretations of each DISC style:

"D" Dominance
How you respond to problems and challenges

Action Orientation: extrovert, takes proactive action, views self as more powerful than the environment

Environment Orientation: task oriented, views world unfavorably

You Will Notice: self-confidence, directness, forcefulness, risk-taking, results orientation

Motivated By: power and authority, competition, winning, success, new challenges

Fears: loss of control, being taken advantage of, vulnerability

Emotion Under Stress: anger

Tone of Voice: strong, clear, confident, fast-paced

Body Language: forward-leaning, hand in pocket, direct eye contact, leans in, walks quickly

Limitations: lacks concern for others, impatience, insensitivity, dislikes routine and details

Conflict or Negotiation Style: competition; assertive, but not cooperative

Strengths: self-starter, tenacious, hard worker, focused on big picture goals

Emails: short, to the point, focused on results

Favorite Reads: executive book summaries

Hobbies: competitive sports, physical activity

Strategies to Influence a "D":
    be efficient and succinct
    flatter their ego
    mention new and innovative products
    emphasize results
    touch high points and the bottom line
    solve problems fast to impress
    offer multiple alternatives

ask questions and for their opinion
don't offer testimonials or opinions
stick to business, don't socialize

If you meet someone who:

- Is ambitious, forceful, independent, innovative, antagonistic, quick to anger, and results-oriented
- Loves change and taking risks, makes quick decisions
- Prefers competitive sports/hobbies
- Reads executive book summaries
- Walks quickly in a straight line
- Has a large desk with many piles
- Uses big nonverbal gestures, multitasks and interrupts frequently

Communicate to him/her by:

- Asking relevant questions
- Being clear, specific, and brief
- Talking win-win
- Not chitchatting, rambling, or repeating yourself
- Not discussing personal things
- Flattering their ego
- Continually referring to results

"I" Influence
How you influence people and contacts to your point of view

Action Orientation: extrovert, takes proactive action, views self as more powerful than the environment
Environment Orientation: people-oriented, views world favorably

You Will Notice: charm, enthusiasm, sociability, optimism, talkativeness, emotional

Motivated By: social recognition, group activities, friendly relationships, freedom from rules

Fears: social rejection, disapproval, loss of influence, being ignored

Emotion Under Stress: optimism

Tone of Voice: animated, friendly, rambling explanations, sense of humor

Body Language: smiles often, uses expressive gestures, weaves when walking

Limitations: oversells, too trusting, situational listener, disorganization, impulsive decisions

Conflict or Negotiation Style: collaboration; assertive, cooperative

Strengths: enthusiasm, team player, thinks outside the box, encourages others, problem resolution

Emails: warm, people focus, wordy

Favorite Reads: fiction and self-improvement

Hobbies: attending events with people

Strategies to Influence an "I":

> mention showy products and services
> socialize first, then talk business
> share personal stories and testimonials
> touch high points
> quick process and close them fast
> stay high level and avoid details
> give them room to talk
> offer a friendly environment
> support their dreams
> offer multiple alternatives
> provide in-depth follow-up
> touch them (professionally)

If you meet someone who:

- Is magnetic, enthusiastic, friendly, optimistic, demonstrative
- Accepts change and taking risks, makes both quick and slow decisions
- Likes interaction with people after a stressful day
- Reads fiction and self-improvement books
- Weaves when walking
- Has a desk with many piles, memorabilia of experiences
- Uses big nonverbal gestures and facial expressions

Communicate to him/her by:

- Providing a warm and friendly environment
- Touching appropriately
- Not discussing details in person
- Asking "feeling" questions
- Praising/recognizing them
- Supporting their dreams
- Dropping names of friends or subject matter experts

"S" Steadiness
How you respond to pace and consistency

Action Orientation: introvert, is reactive, views self as less powerful than the environment
Environment Orientation: people-oriented, views world favorably
You Will Notice: patience, team player, calm approach, good listener, humility, sympathetic

Motivated By: stable environments, sincere appreciation, cooperation, opportunities to help, safety

Fears: loss of stability, change, loss of harmony, offending others

Emotion Under Stress: non-emotional

Tone of Voice: low tone, warm, methodical

Body Language: small gestures, relaxed, leans back, walks with an easy pace

Limitations: overly accommodating, tendency to avoid change, indecisiveness, possessiveness

Conflict or Negotiation Style: accommodation; not assertive, cooperative

Strengths: active listener, task finisher, patient, compliant with authority

Emails: long with considerable information

Favorite Reads: popular, fiction and nonfiction

Hobbies: being alone, resting

Strategies to Influence a "S":

> mention traditional products
> trust you before you can close them
> support them making family-oriented decisions
> provide a slow and easy process
> do not hard sell
> offer repeated visits to build trust
> offer additional time to think through
> show how it's the complete solution
> give assurances, facts, and data

If you meet someone who:

- Is patient, predictable, reliable, steady, modest
- Follows rules, needs to prepare for and doesn't like change; makes decisions slowly

- After a long day, wants rest/sleep
- Reads popular stories, fiction and nonfiction
- Walks in a steady, easy pace
- Office feels very homey, family portraits
- Small hand gestures, leans back, hands in pockets

Communicate to him/her by:

- Breaking the ice with personal small talk
- Presenting nonthreateningly, quietly, and logically
- Asking "how" questions with time to think
- Showing interest in them as a person
- Involving their family, avoiding hard sells
- Detailing how an idea is a complete solution

"C" Compliance
How you respond to procedures and constraints

Action Orientation: introvert, is reactive, views self as less powerful than the environment

Environment Orientation: task-oriented, views the world unfavorably

You Will Notice: precision, analysis, skepticism, reserve, quiet

Motivated By: uses expertise or gaining knowledge, attention to quality, completing projects

Fears: criticism, sloppy methods, being wrong

Emotion Under Stress: fear

Tone of Voice: monotone, precise, deliberate

Body Language: direct eye contact, little to no gestures, walks in straight line, arms folded, hand on chin

Limitations: overly critical, tendency to overanalyze, isolates self, defensive

Conflict or Negotiation Style: avoid interaction; not assertive, not cooperative

Strengths: high standards, accurate, diplomatic, detail-oriented, effective troubleshooter

Emails: direct with appropriate data

Favorite Reads: technical journals, nonfiction

Hobbies: being alone

Strategies to Influence a "C":
> mention proven products and services
> show connection to what's tried and true
> provide a slow and easy process
> don't hard sell
> offer additional time to think through
> give assurances, facts, and data
> emphasize losses by delaying choice
> answer questions thoroughly
> provide background information
> minimize their risk, offer security

If you meet someone who:

- Is dependent, neat, conservative, perfectionist, compliant
- Dislikes risk-taking and change
- Relieves stress by being alone
- Reads nonfiction technical journals
- Walks in a straight line
- Has an office that is very functional with graphs and charts
- Uses little to no gestures, arms folded, one hand on chin

Communicate to him/her by:

- Presenting nonthreateningly, quietly, and logically
- Explaining details to minimize risk
- Emphasizing losses caused by delay
- Not overpromising but instead focusing on security
- Avoiding the hard sell and instead offering time to digest facts

12 Driving Forces: 2 of 5

The second TTISI assessment I use is the 12 Driving Forces assessment.[30] It is different from the DISC in that the 12 Driving Forces reveals unobservable subconscious motivators guiding our conscious choices. When we live life doing things in alignment with our motivators, we're happy, engaged, and in a state of flow.[31] On the 12 Driving Forces report, TTISI places each of the 12 motivators into three buckets (primary, situational, indifferent) based upon how important the motivator is to you. When coaching, I ask clients to focus on their top four, their primary driving forces.

When talking through someone's top four motivators, I often ask what percentage of the day they're able to live that motivator. If they're unable to live the motivator often, we brainstorm ways it can be introduced more into their lives. Happiness and alignment are born out of doing things that are meaningful to you. When you're in a job, relationship, or community group that doesn't allow you to be your authentic self, you'd be well-served to begin conversations to understand how you can find more time living what's most important to you.

If you don't know what your top four driving forces are, consider contacting TTISI for access to the assessment. Based on my experiences, here are my interpretations of the 12 Driving Forces.

Instinctive: People who are driven by utilizing past experience, intuition, and seeking specific knowledge when necessary. They rely on past experiences and start projects before having all the necessary information.

Intellectual: People who are driven by opportunities to learn, acquire knowledge, and discover truth. They will research until all information is discovered before starting a project.

Selfless: People who are driven by completing tasks for the sake of completion, with little expectation of personal return. They focus on the greater good and value people for who they are versus what they can provide.

Resourceful: People who are driven by practical results, maximizing both efficiency and returns for their investments of time, talent, energy, and resources. They're driven to maximize opportunities to create financial flexibility and energized building frameworks that maximize their investment in projects.

Objective: People who are driven by the functionality and objectivity of their surroundings. They see the world in pieces, not as a whole, and thrive in a chaos-filled environment.

Harmonious: People who are driven by the experience, subjective viewpoints, and balance in their surroundings. They focus on the totality of a situation and enjoy creating rapport and tranquility with others.

Intentional: People who are driven to assist others for a specific purpose, not just for the sake of being helpful or supportive. They see the world as a toolset to accomplish their goals and keep emotion out of business decisions.

Altruistic: People who are driven to assist others for the satisfaction of being helpful or supportive. They instinctively notice and respond to those in need and believe people should have the opportunity to be the best they can be.

Collaborative: People who are driven by being in a supporting role and contributing with little need for individual recognition. They focus on the greater good, not advancing their position, and enjoy being behind the scenes to get things done.

Commanding: People who are driven by status, recognition, and control over personal freedom. They work long and hard to advance their position and desire to create something that leads to an enduring legacy.

Receptive: People who are driven by new ideas, methods, and opportunities that fall outside a defined system for living. They seek new ways to accomplish routine tasks and like to set their own plan to guide their actions.

Structured: People who are driven by traditional approaches, proven methods, and a defined system for living. They will work diligently to advance causes they believe in and value following tried and true systems.

There is no right or wrong combination of motivators. The key is knowing what your top four are and then living them an increasing percentage of the day. Would an Intellectual person love working for a university? Yes. Would a Resourceful person be happy working year after year for free? No. Would a Harmonious person enjoy working in an ever-changing startup? No. Would a Collaborative person love being an administrative assistant? Yes. Would a Receptive person thrive in a sales role? Yes. The key is knowing your preference and aligning your life with opportunities to live that preference.

Identifying Your Core Values: 3 of 5

This may be the most important piece of the self-discovery puzzle. Western societies don't often encourage people to uncover their life missions, core values, motivators, deeper levels of emotional intelligence, etc. That's unfortunate because one of the fastest ways to realign your behavior and hold yourself accountable to live out your Earth school curriculum is to overtly name your top core values.

When you are living in alignment with your core values, you will feel more engaged, supported, and in flow. There is a great deal of payoff in defining your values, connecting them to your organization's core values, and choosing daily actions that ensure you are living them more. Understanding one another's core values is a great opportunity for increasing empathy and improving communication. Groups with shared core values enjoy greater cohesion and goal alignment. One great tool for helping to do this is the PEAK Values Card Deck.[32] Each card has a different human core value, a descriptive picture, and synonyms that offer further insight.

Conflict is often born out of taking action that is in opposition to someone else's core values. There may be many other causes, yet this seems to be one where people can understand why they feel emotionally triggered. They begin to realize the other person likely wasn't trying to hurt them. They begin taking ownership of their feelings and can more easily describe how what the other person did violated their values. Lines of communication and understanding open.

Whether you use the PEAK Values Card Deck or another tool, methodically reflecting on your life's experiences and whittling a large number of possible core values down to your top six is empowering. I also encourage you to force rank your top six.[33]

If you look at your top core values and realize you're not spending much time living them day to day, here's an activity you can do alone. On a sheet of paper, write each value in order vertically down the left-hand margin. Next, for each value, ask yourself, "In what new ways can I live this value?" Write as many ideas as you can. Most people don't do this. You may need a trusted friend to brainstorm with you. Regardless of how you make your list, it will open your eyes to possibility.

I've included a summary of my core values and how I live each of them later on in this chapter, so you'll have a better idea of what I mean.

I've also partnered with clients to help them find the connection between their personal core values and their employers' values. On a sheet of paper, write your personal values in order vertically down the left-hand margin. Next, look at your employer's values and attempt to find commonality. If there is a link, write your employer's value or phrase just to the right of your matching value. Repeat this as many times as you feel called to. Hopefully, you find many links.

Once you do this, you will start seeing how you can feel a deeper level of connection between yourself and the "why" of the organization you work with. In some cases, I ask clients to write a third column filled with specific examples of what they tangibly do at work that allows them to live their personal values and the organization's values simultaneously. This is a powerful employee engagement and retention tool. But it can also lead to someone moving on from a role, and that's fine, too. As someone aligns with their curriculum, changes will occur.

Past, Present, and Future Questions: 4 of 5

In addition to learning about their observable behavior from the DISC, subconscious motivators from the 12 Driving Forces, and lessons learned represented by your core values, I realized clients needed an easier way to see how their childhood years shaped their daily habits today. The following questions purposely review your past's highs and lows, how you spend your time today, and where you'd like to invest time in the future. This is the Q&A that Avni found particularly helpful in our work together.

PAST

These questions are designed to identify transformative experiences from your early years. There is no right or wrong answer. I want you to respond to these questions with as much depth as possible. The more you express your feelings, who was involved, the sequence of events, etc., the easier it will be to see patterns when you reflect later.

What is your favorite childhood memory?

What was the most trying experience in your life?

What did you learn about yourself or our world while traveling?

What did you love to do in your free time?

Is there a cause you've devoted time to and felt passionate about?

What are the most important life lessons you've learned?

Are there perceived problems or issues that have occurred repeatedly?

What things did you want to be remembered for?

What did you think you'd do if you had unlimited money and could not fail?

PRESENT

Now think about your present job. Be honest with yourself about the situation and what you like and dislike. Again, any and all responses are welcome. The more detail and depth you offer, the easier it will be later to write your guiding statements. Think of your responses as a baseline by which you can look at your life.

Activities you spend the most time on
(e.g., email, meetings, employee management, job duties)

Activities that interest you
(e.g., things at work that excite you, give you energy,
what you work extra for)

Location of your office
(e.g., how long your commute is, in major metro area/
small town, size of office)

Total compensation
(e.g., salary, bonus, benefits, retirement, travel, expense
account)

Daily tasks
(e.g., sales calls, spreadsheet analysis, strategic thinking,
team projects)

Responsibility level
(e.g., your title, size of budget, number of direct reports)

Growth potential
(e.g., promotion after X years, additional professional
development opportunities)

FUTURE

Next, choose a date three to five years from today. Invest time
into visualizing what your ideal life will look and feel like.
Then, with that visual kept in your mind, offer responses to
the following statements.

Activities you'd prefer to spend the most time on

Location of your office

Total compensation

Daily tasks

Responsibility level

Growth potential

If you look at your responses for Present and Future, do you see differences? A gap between where you are and where you'd like to be? This gap will be helpful in defining your goals.

Your Authority: 5 of 5

Some people struggle when looking at themselves objectively, understanding who they really are, and seeing themselves as capable. By inviting you to explore your past and identify your accomplishments, awards, wins, recognitions, publications, etc., I want you to feel empowered. From present to past, make a list of things you're proud of. These can include degrees, certifications, board positions, classes taken, volunteerism, life experiences, businesses built/bought/sold, projects at work, and more.

If you struggle to complete this activity, consider: What are some ways you've added value or bettered other lives? Think through why others consider you an expert. What are your top professional strengths? I'm guessing you're not going to want to brag; I understand you wish to remain humble. But now is the time to see yourself in a new light. List as many things you're proud of as possible.

Find Your Patterns

Using the information gathered from your DISC, the 12 Driving Forces, your core values, the past, present, and future questions, and your authority list, invest time in reflection. Gather your reports and your notes. Place the five in front of you, grab a sheet of paper, and begin identifying currents, feelings, and themes. Can you find similar language inside your DISC report and in one of your top core values? Does one of your core values connect with the answer you provided about past lessons learned? Maybe one of your driving forces seems quite similar to one of your values? What commonality do you see in your DISC style and an accomplishment on your authority list? Did one of your authority list accomplishments happen because of a past travel experience?

This will likely be the hardest component of the process for people to complete. It requires time for you to be still. Crash disparate ideas together. See connections you didn't know existed previously. If you look closely at the five tools, from piece to piece, there are going to be words, ideas, and connections that repeatedly show up. Your goal is to find six to eight patterns where you found examples across two to three of your five tools.

Once you have six to eight patterns, you'll then use those to draft your guiding statements: your mission, your value proposition, and your goals.

Your Personal Mission

What makes you different?

What makes you unique?

How can you help others?

What is your "why," your life's purpose?

Your answers to these questions help to form your personal mission statement. A simple way to think about this is to review your answers to the past questions about your life's biggest challenge and your recurring challenges. At some point around age 28, you found a way to overcome those challenges using lessons you learned. Now your life will have deep meaning and be closely aligned with your curriculum if you help others overcome the same challenge for themselves that you overcame.

I was not allowed to be my authentic self while living in Michigan. While a student at Thunderbird, I awakened to my true self, and my coaching practice is built upon helping others become the most authentic and aligned versions of themselves.

I wasn't authentic. I learned how to be authentic. I help others become authentic.

My mission is "I exist to unlock human potential through the development of personal and professional well-being."

I believe you can readily apply this equation to your life. Draft a one-sentence, easy-to-repeat, simple-to-understand personal mission statement. Ask close friends and family if it represents you. Sit on it for 30–60 days. Eventually, the universe will confirm that it's right for you.

Here are examples:

I am a coach who uses outdoor activities and life's adventures to develop a community of close-knit relationships to serve those in need.

I am a mentor who uses business frameworks and unique learning experiences to improve others' economic opportunities.

I exist to create environments that break people free from self-limiting beliefs and traditional structures.

Your Value Proposition

You've gathered considerable information about your journey. You've identified enduring patterns. You've drafted a one-sentence mission statement. Now you want to highlight the most important pieces to display how you add value to others, your organization, and community. Envision this being used at the top of your resume, in your LinkedIn summary, or in an executive biography. If you don't feel comfortable writing this yourself, find a friend or colleague who can assist. I want you to feel safe trying. Your goal is to include language from your six to eight themes with specific examples pulled from your five tools.

Here are three examples of clients who have invested time to write out their value propositions.

1. Sarah is an experienced senior financial executive, CPA, and EMBA with deep expertise in financial modeling, product pricing analysis, and streamlining operations' processes. An optimistic mentor who motivates

and leads high-performing teams to achieve big results, she builds frameworks to maximize efficiency and excel in purpose-driven companies. A continual learner and growth-oriented leader who is resilient and works hard to drive meaningful return on investment, Sarah solves problems creatively and openly shares knowledge and appreciation. She is active in multiple professional associations and community-based philanthropic endeavors.

2. Avni is a vice president who delivers innovative results leading multimillion-dollar product portfolios and global teams for B2B and B2C organizations. Her expertise is in solving complex business and change management opportunities through connecting people, data, analytics, and technology for geographically dispersed and highly matrixed groups. An executive who transforms processes to drive value for customers, grow revenue, and increase profitability, Avni is a courageous, compassionate, and empathetic leader who has launched new products in Australia, North America, Asia, and Europe in ever-changing marketplaces. She has a track record of building transparent relationships, promoting cross-group collaboration, developing world-class talent, and leading highly engaged teams. A continual learner who holds a master's in global management and a master's in economics and who is a certified SAFe 4 Agilist, Avni is an influencer who creates innovative experiences and reinforces empowering beliefs that encourage lifelong learning, enable self-expression, and connect people for growth and fulfilling lives.

3. John is independent and is fiercely loyal. He is competitive, driven by integrity, and comfortable making high-risk decisions, and he takes an unconventional

approach to goal achievement. John builds frameworks and facilitates important relationships to produce excellent business outcomes. He is a mentor and coach who achieves big goals through people. John is a continual learner who repeatedly questions traditions to create unique solutions. He loves travel and outdoor recreation. John actively gives time to community programs and loves health and wellness. He is a devoted husband and proud father of three adult children.

Your Goals

The work you're doing to know yourself more deeply will realign your life. It'll reconnect you with your Earth school curriculum. How you set and work toward your goals matters a great deal. I encourage you to review the answers you offered in the Present and Future sections of the Q&A. Examine the gaps and design your annual goals based on them.

I recommend your goals be metrics-driven and have a due date. The format I prefer to use is "From X to Y by When." I first learned of this in Chris McChesney's book *The Four Disciplines of Execution*.[34] Where you are now: X. Where you want to be: Y. What date you will be done: When.

Think of your potential goals as fitting into one of three buckets: personal, professional, and relationship. Here are some examples:

- By January 1st, 2024, my personal income will increase from $100,000 to $250,000.
- Before July 31st, 2022, I will complete an Ironman race.

- By December 31st, 2021, my husband and I will visit five new National Parks.

The point of metrics-based goals is to say unemotionally, objectively, and unequivocally that you either did or did not accomplish the goal.

No matter what goals you choose, I want you to feel empowered to honor new levels of accountability and ownership of your life's choices. We will explore the idea of breaking your goals into weekly habits more fully in part three.

Living My Own Core Values and Life's Mission

My choice to go to back to school for an MBA—the roots of discovering my own life's mission and value proposition—was born out of a place of lack. In 2007, as things slowed in the economy, vacancy rose and timeshare sales dropped at the resort where I worked. My boss and I tried a variety of tactics to turn things around, but we both saw the writing on the wall and we resigned at the same time.

I decided to work for my dad again, managing the books remotely, putting together estimates for clients, and developing new human resources processes. Although we still didn't see eye to eye, I'm grateful he welcomed me back into his business. The calling for a life filled with travel became stronger. I started researching MBA programs and discovered Arizona State University had an international MBA program. I attended one of their sessions, applied, and was accepted.

A couple of weeks later, I attended a party at a friend's house—a friend I hadn't seen in years—and struck up a conversation with a man I'd never met. As the conversation progressed, I mentioned that I had recently been accepted into the international business program at ASU. The gentleman said, "Have you heard of the Thunderbird School of Global Management?"

I honestly hadn't, even though I lived less than three miles from the school's campus. Later that evening, I visited their website and discovered they were having a preview weekend the following month. I registered. The day after attending the preview, I submitted an application. Their enrollment team interviewed me. I had no business getting into the school based on my body of work and lack of international experiences. I was not their traditional candidate. But they knew I was willing to pay full tuition. I decided to become a full-time student. I didn't realize it at the time, but it was meant to be.

On the Friday before classes were to start, Kasen told me she was leaving. We'd need to sell the house, divide assets, and begin anew separate. For some reason, I was being realigned with my Earth school curriculum, and Thunderbird was the place I'd take off. It doesn't always feel like it, but the universe is always guiding us. It's always conspiring for your success.

I went through an awakening process while a student at Thunderbird with the help of a coach named Pam. Pam was the first person I'd ever encountered who not only asked me what I actually wanted to do with my life . . . but then gave me a process for how to awaken to it. Pam asked me to complete DISC, 12 Driving Forces, CareerLeader, and StrengthsFinder 2.0. We then sat down and went through the results, and she showed me—one by one—what each meant, how it could be applied, and how a specific career would use my strengths and be engaging to me.

I think this was the first time I truly realized that I didn't need to emulate someone else's path. Instead, I needed to explore "data" about myself for the answers. The more I gathered data about me, the more the path became clear. Pam was an angel in my life. My brain always liked linear processes. She showed me that awakening to your authenticity IS a linear process.

I processed my feelings of loss. I overcame fear. I released emotions. I recognized my life's challenges and found a way to overcome them. I traveled to China. I learned to speak Mandarin. I met incredible people. Gradually, I uncovered my life's mission.

In an effort to be vulnerable and connect to my life's core values, I want to share my list with you to help overcome my fears of telling my own story. They are:

1. Authenticity
2. Growth
3. Spirituality
4. Wellness
5. Money
6. Power

My first core value is authenticity. As I thought about the last 10 to 15 years, I asked myself, "What have I done that has been really authentically me?" I realized moving from Montague to Phoenix was an authentic choice because nobody in my extended family lives outside of Michigan. I own a small business as opposed to working for a large corporation. It's important to me to have control over my time and destiny. Running a business and being able to control what I do day to day feels authentic.

I share my story on my website, social media, speaking engagements, and other mediums because it teaches me about myself. It helps me lead by example and give others a feeling of confidence that they can share their story vulnerably without shame. It's something those close to me rarely do, but it's something I think is important so I do it, even though the potential for criticism is high.

When it comes to everyday choices such as clothing, I avoid wearing suits and ties. Back in the '70s, '80s, and '90s, if you worked corporate, you needed to wear a suit and tie. Being authentic to me means wearing untraditional shoes, a pair of jeans, a T-shirt, and a sport coat. Next-generation leadership means honoring the previous generation's norms, yet offering an authentic version of yourself that fits the society of today. I have hats embroidered with my name and business logo. No matter where I am, I'm sharing my beliefs proudly. I rarely wear hats from other brands. Why would I advertise for that company without getting paid? Some people wear others' brand names because they feel an emotional connection to that company or sports team or celebrity. I respect that. But this book is about breaking the Piscean connection to believing in an outside authority and forming an Aquarian connection to deeply believing in yourself. "I know that *I* have the answers."

Another example is in the way I listen actively. I've been told there are few people as present as I am when I'm with another person. In all those years in emotional isolation on the farm, I promised myself one day I'd be a great listener and be truly present for others. I want them to feel heard and understood in ways I wasn't. It feels like a gift I can offer them. Doing this for others also heals me as I learn more about myself through their stories. They may not know it, but their journeys mirror back to me what I've learned and what I need to begin working on.

My second core value is growth. I've hired four executive coaches to guide me in transforming pieces of my business. I've hired three Reiki masters to help shed emotional traumas. I've worked with a psychic to understand past lives and what may be coming. I've interacted with energy healers. It takes faith and trust to lower my walls and open my eyes to what these souls have to share with me. To me, growth can come from traditional coaching and education models, but it happens faster from nontraditional sources such as energy healing.

Words don't teach. Experiences do.

A big catalyst for my growth is my daily journal. Some days the journal is simply what I did that day or how many calories I burned at the gym. More often than not it's details of what I learned, what I'm grateful for, or what I felt. On the first of the month, I have a three-hour time block that affords me mental time to read the previous month's entries. I search for patterns and attempt to adjust my habits for the coming month. I notice quickly when what used to emotionally trigger me no longer triggers me. That may be the ultimate sign of growth for anyone: if what used to bother us emotionally no longer does. As time passes, you'll notice you move from feeling bothered to moving through the bother faster to not being bothered at all.

International travel has also been important for my evolution. Each trip offers me a different perspective and helps me see other approaches to life. Learning to speak Mandarin was an enormous period of growth because I was able to see why Chinese culture is constructed the way it is. When I began dreaming in Mandarin, I realized how much I was growing—I was tapping into parts of my soul I didn't know existed before.

My third core value is spirituality. Each morning for 20 minutes, I sit in meditation. It's foundational for me to find balance, knowing that I'll bring calm energy to the day and that I stay closer to my curriculum when grounded to Earth.

Initially, my spiritual growth happened through traditional counseling, talking through what I was feeling or experiencing. The more I talked through different events, the more I understood the underlying emotion the event was bringing to the surface for me to release and heal. This allowed me to take control and not let outside forces control my emotions. You gain immense power when you stop blaming others and regulate your emotional response. Meditation is about management of my energy, aligning with the Schumann resonance, and balancing emotions.[35]

Patricia gifted me a card deck and book entitled *Medicine Cards*.[36] It shares stories and different meanings Native Americans associated with 52 Earth animals. In our time together, she would ask about animals I saw repeatedly. We talked through the metaphorical meaning of the animal and how it applied to lessons I was learning. It was beyond helpful. When I'm about to have a hard conversation, I pull one of the Medicine Cards and try to use that animal's energy to guide the conversation in a way that best serves who I am helping.

Another energy healer taught me to recognize patterns, specifically in numbers. She asked, "Do you see numbers repeating on license plates, clocks, or on computer screens?" I realized I did. In numerology and astrology, numbers and combinations of numbers have specific meanings.[37] As I've aligned more with my curriculum, I've learned to recognize a pattern and apply its meaning to my circumstances to help me make on-the-spot adjustments. For example, seeing "555" suggests that a change is headed your way. When I see that number multiple times, I know something in my life is about to change. Instead of trying to control the change, I simply accept it.

I have a small crystal pendant. To quality-check how aligned I am, I lie down and dangle the pendant over each of my seven chakras one by one, as explained by Robert Bruce in his book *Astral Dynamics*.[38] The more it rotates, the more that chakra is open. If it does not rotate, the energy center or chakra is blocked. I then sit in meditation thinking through that chakra's purpose in the human body, what's happening in my life, and what I'd need to do to release old emotions and open the chakra.

Finally, I spend more time in nature than I used to. It offers me deeper levels of emotional safety, calm, and clarity. If I kayak, hike, or swim, I feel my energy recalibrate to the Schumann resonance. I'm continually looking for unconventional opportunities that give me further learning and understanding of the world and that allow me to envision the life I want while figuring out how I will impact the world.

Wellness is my fourth core value. Once per day, I'm physically active. I hike, play a round of golf, or attend an instructor-led class at the gym. I choose to eat vegetarian. I don't eat meat and avoid most processed animal proteins such as eggs, cheese, or milk. In my childhood, I ate a lot of dairy products and processed foods. I struggled with allergies, a biliary disease, and extra weight. I caught colds and the flu regularly.

In 2017, I completed the 23andMe genetic assessment and asked the physicians at the Boulder Longevity Institute to decode my genome to offer food, supplement, and exercise recommendations.[39] It's transformed my life. I don't feel pain in the ways I used to. My cells are not as inflamed. I build muscle quickly, burn unwanted fat faster, and have higher levels of energy. It's amazing what small dietary changes can do to give my body the customized nutrients it needs.

I also shy away from wheat-based products as I have genetic markers for celiac disease. I choose to eat foods like dark greens, plant-based proteins, almond milk, and dark berries to create an alkaline and oxygenated environment in my blood. I fast each week to give my body time to not process food but to focus on repairing and healing itself.

My body functions well on a seven- to eight-hour rest. My body doesn't produce it well, so I take melatonin each night. Not only do our bodies recover while we sleep, but we dream. We can learn much metaphorically from our dreams. When I wake up, I search the Dream Moods app[40] to help me understand what the subconscious dream was trying to teach my conscious self. I journal what I learned and continue to identify patterns to keep me emotionally balanced.

My last two values are power and wealth. Some perceive power as the desire to have control over other people. To me, power is having complete control over how I distribute my time. In running a small business, I'm able to live this value in choosing what clients I work with, what projects I participate in, or what community organizations I donate time to.

Traditionalists and baby boomers were raised at a time in human history where it was commonplace to work for the same corporation an entire career. And when they retired, that company continued to provide for them via retirement or pension plans. In retirement, they had time to do the activities they enjoyed most. For Generations X, Y, and Z, those financial safety nets will not exist. Although employers are no longer responsible for your retirement, you now have the freedom to change jobs, take sabbaticals, and travel anytime you'd like.

You don't have to wait for retirement to live life.

You can have unique experiences while you're young and physically able. I value the power inherent in the ability to have unique experiences when I desire and not at some future date that may never arrive.

As I wrote earlier, never having been taught how to budget was hard for me. Much of my curriculum around wealth has been trying to shed what I learned emulating my father's belief that wealth was the only thing that mattered. I needed to release the mindset that having wealth is what made someone important. I now honor the freedom money provides and the ways it allows me to uplift my community. I now see it as safety, adding value to others' lives, and creating opportunities that didn't exist before. This was an unbelievably hard transition for me to make.

Today, I feel beyond blessed. I live comfortably. I'm conscious of my budget and live simply so I can grow my savings and investments. I enjoy making money and being rewarded with solid returns on investment for my expertise. The more money I make, the more people I can uplift.

Your Saturn Return

When I'm asked for a shorter equation to uncover someone's mission, I explain these three pain-to-purpose journey steps:

1. First, you endure a challenge.
2. Next, you overcome the challenge.
3. Then, you help other people overcome that same challenge.

In Super Bowl 51, the underdogs, the Atlanta Falcons, were winning 28 to 0 at halftime. The New England Patriots were down by four touchdowns. They could've just given up. But instead, they used the break to adjust their plans. They made tweaks to their game plan and they paid off. The Patriots won 34 to 28.

I'm not a fan of football, but it continually strikes me that even though nothing went their way in the first half, the Patriots designed a new approach at halftime that turned their fortunes around in the second half. In much the same way, we can overcome challenges and turn things around in our lives.

In the second half, the Patriots did most everything right. The Falcons did nearly everything wrong. If the game had been relatively close in the first half, the Patriots might not have adjusted their game plan and they might have lost the game. Because the challenge was so profound, they had little choice but to make big adjustments.

Around the ages of 28 and 48, approximately, every human has what astrologers call a "Saturn Return." When Saturn enters the same astrological alignment that it was in when that person was born, that person is put in a reflective state to think through their life's previous phase. Some people call it the quarter-life crisis around age 28. Some call it the midlife crisis around age 48. The point of each Saturn return, or the loose metaphorical equivalent to my halftime example, is that if you reflect on your life's previous phase and you want to make a big adjustment to get back in alignment with your curriculum, the time is now.

Now that you've taken the time to discover the values, motivators, and goals powering your life's mission, you can take the next step on the *I Know* journey: building your emotional intelligence.

Key Takeaways

- You are blessed and have more blessings coming. It is time for you to flourish.
- Let's be equal, yet different. Let's do less, yet better. Focus on the now, together.
- If you've lived relatively close to your soul's Earth school curriculum, the Saturn Return may be less challenging.
- As change occurs on Earth, 95% of your life will remain the same. In the stillness, focus on what is unchanged.
- Living authentically means getting to know yourself—not the self you've been told you are but the self you really are.
- Getting into the flow of change means no longer acting simply for personal empowerment. It means operating in a way where you add value to everyone you meet.
- Validated assessments help us understand how we can best interact with the world, know what to say "yes" or "no" to, and see others without judgment.

- Each D, I, S, and C style has default action orientations, motivations, fears, emotions under stress, conflict styles, and more.
- Each 12 Driving Forces style offers a window into our subconscious, unobservable motivations.
- Understanding others and what drives them removes a barrier of communication to allow you to thrive collaboratively.
- Western education systems don't teach people what their core values are. You have to uncover them for yourself.
- The gap between your present and future states is the foundation of your goals.
- By completing the five tools and identifying your life's themes, you're proactively designing a plan to realign with your Earth school curriculum.
- Even when it doesn't feel like it, the universe is always guiding you.
- In most cases, you can't control change; you can only control your response to it.
- Our pain-to-purpose journey includes enduring a challenge, overcoming that challenge, and then helping others overcome that same challenge for themselves.

Chapter 5:
Emotional
Intelligence

Perfection is the lowest standard you can set. ~Michael S.
Seaver

My stepdaughter Aleah was born in a small Montana town. An only child, she is an incredibly advanced and old soul. From the time I met her in 2013, she has been independent, wanting to do things her way. She is not a fan of traditional education. She doesn't accept the status quo.

At different times in her life, she loved shopping at second-hand stores. She enjoyed being in nature. She enjoys concerts and music festivals—it's as if she's a 1960s hippie in the 21st century. She adores Stevie Nicks and adopted a cat—which she named Stevie—that is missing its tail and front right leg. She proudly displays multiple tattoos.

Aleah is a collectivist, a person who challenges the mainstream, a person who likes to share her journey authentically with others. She uses music and energy to create memorable experiences. She lives in the moment and does the things her intuition guides her to. Even if she knows something detrimental might happen, she still wants to try it because she longs for the experience. As her parents or I attempt to guide her, she's likely to go down the path she desires to traverse.

That's the thing I genuinely appreciate most about her: she's completely herself. Aleah is willing to endure short-term pain to meet her most authentic self-worth. She prioritizes unique experiences as central to her Earth school curriculum. She'll try things that are uncomfortable for others, such as recording herself singing, participating in peaceful protests, or living as a vegan simply to feel the emotions of it. Aleah assesses her energy from the event and chooses to continue doing it or not, no matter what anyone says. The internal fortitude she has to be different and deflect others' opinions and judgment is profound.

Aleah and I didn't get along when I first began dating her mother. I'm a rule follower and she isn't. I was trying to get her to ingratiate herself into society; she was purposely trying to do the opposite. For example, she begged her mom and I to adopt a dog and promised she'd do everything to care for it. After one week of him being in the house, Aleah stopped doing all her chores. Me having to constantly remind her wedged us apart. I forgot she was an irrational teenager.

Aleah had a group of friends who encouraged her to do things she didn't feel comfortable doing, but she'd do them anyway to gain acceptance. She broke a window screen on her bedroom window to leave the house late one night; she didn't turn in countless homework assignments. I couldn't understand why she'd agree to one set of rules and then break them week after week; I could never find the right words to ask the right questions that would help me see her perspective, her reasoning . . . I wish I would've.

We had these brief' moments of conflict as I was attempting to parent her in the same way I was parented and she was attempting to experiment, blossom, and fly to her life's next level.

Aleah's major challenge in life is building trusting relationships[41]—figuring out who to trust and how to trust them. She and her dad don't see eye to eye on many topics and trust seems fragile. Her early relationships with romantic partners were surfacy. I often wonder if a deep level of trust existed for her with her dad between birth and age seven—the period of time when our brains are in theta brainwave state and are subconsciously setting life-long habits.

I believe the reason she was brought into my life and I into hers is that we both have the common experience of our father not being there for us in the ways we would've liked them to be. We've spent a disproportionate amount of time looking for trusting, loving, and caring relationships. I've learned so much about authenticity, individuality, and following my heart from Aleah. I hope I've taught her that there *can* be positive male figures who genuinely appreciate her and will show up for her unconditionally.

There's so much we are learning from each other as we're concurrently healing wounds.

Likely my favorite moment with Aleah occurred in 2018 when we got matching tattoos. She asked me to get them while we were backpacking across Europe to celebrate her high school graduation. We were in Munich, Germany. Aleah wanted her first tattoos to have spiritual significance, so she and I have artwork on the inside of our biceps: on the right arm, our sign in the zodiac (me, Pisces; her, Sagittarius). Our left arms feature our ruling planets (me, Neptune; her, Jupiter).[42] We went to the tattoo parlor together, and when I was having mine done, she offered to hold my hand. It melted my heart.

It was an experience she hadn't had before, and it had deep meaning for her. It connects her and me for the rest of our human lives, and it inspired me to want more tattoos. When Aleah asked to hold my hand, it was so comforting. The experience of feeling pain and then automatically being comforted will always stick in my mind. The tattoos are symbolic of what I'm trying to accomplish in my work as well. When I think about how important self-expression has become to me, I ask myself, "How do I lead by example?" I want to show people that a leader can be very business smart, well-spoken, and analytical and can look every bit the traditional leader—and still have a whole sleeve of tattoos if he wants to.

I seek to lead by example and inspire you to do something authentic for yourself. It doesn't have to be collecting tattoos, as long as it's a choice that gives you feelings of clarity.

Test Your Mission

It's through our connections with others, whether it's formal coaching or a personal relationship like the one I enjoy with Aleah, that we become more of ourselves. The tools and examples I introduced in the last chapter are important during this discovery process, and I hope you dove into them and found a new level of clarity. Now that you're clear on your mission statement, core values, value proposition, and a set of goals, it's time to test those things. Ask yourself, "Am I doing activities that are aligning with my mission, my core values?"

It all comes down to *where you invest your time.*

Thanks to free will, there are specific actions you can take to make the emotionally painful process of getting back to your Earth school curriculum easier, faster, and less painful. These tactics can be learned and taught to others.

Interruptions occur daily and can come from seemingly limitless sources including family, colleagues, clients, technology, the environment you're in, and more. When you are challenged with where to distribute time, choosing what to say yes or no to can cause anxiety. Getting closer to your Earth school curriculum—if you're currently off of it—takes time.

As for Aleah, over the next decade, I think she'll continue to seek unique experiences. During her first Saturn Return, she'll uncover a higher level of true confidence within herself. She's a gifted Reiki practitioner but doesn't yet pursue it strongly. In offering other types of energetic healing for people, she's talked about serving others as a doula, helping women bring children into our world. Her relationship with her dad will improve. Around age 30, she'll likely start her own family and launch her own business healing others' energy and helping them build trusting relationships with those close to them.

How Are You Spending Your Time?

Life is not a one-tank journey.

There will be several versions of you—before and after a Saturn Return, through each of Jung's four life stages (more on this in chapter 6), and as you experience the ups and downs of Campbell's hero's journey for yourself. Maybe you're a kinesthetic learner and like the thought of beta testing activities you're considering inviting into your life more. After you've tested and experienced the activity three or four times, you'll have a deeper understanding of how your life may evolve. You'll be able to say yes or no.

After cycling through these questions and ideas, you should sense a feeling, an alignment for or against a specific course of action. You can now begin making minor changes to where you give your time. Your schedule is opening to productive, value-added activities.

Here are questions you can ask about any activity or course of action you're considering—personally or professionally—to make sure you're consciously moving in alignment with your curriculum:

> How closely aligned with my personal mission statement is the activity?

> How does this activity align with and help me live my personal core values?

> How does investing time into this allow me to communicate authentically and in alignment with my behavioral profile?

> How will this activity allow me to live one or more of my motivators?

> In what ways will this activity allow me to leverage my professional strengths?

What is the connection between this activity and my individual goals?

After reflecting on this choice, what are the tangible advantages and disadvantages of potential outcomes?

What personal risks are associated with this activity?

Decision-Making Tools

The following tools help you know when to say yes or no. This material is foundational as you begin realigning your life with the guiding statements written in the previous chapter.

When reflecting on a person you interacted with or an activity you participated in, assess your body's level of energy. High energy can be associated with feelings of happiness, joy, love, acceptance, and a yearning for more. The interaction gave you energy. It was uplifting and you'd like to invite more of it into your life. If you felt sadness, anger, grief, envy, or exhaustion, your body's energy was low. Your energy was drained or extracted from you. You question whether you want to do that thing again. Or you may benefit from having a conversation with an important person to find win-win solutions.

Did the person extract or give you energy?

Were you in "flow" where the rest of the world shut off and you lost track of time?

Interruptions and opportunities are always around us. I've learned you have to give up the good to welcome in and allow the great into your life. When you begin choosing what work projects, boards of directors, nonprofit organizations, and entrepreneurial ventures to pursue, you should see a strong correlation between its purpose, values, and goals and your personal mission, core values, and goals. If you can't see the connection, say no. If you see a fit, wonderful. Then ask yourself more detailed questions.

What new skills will I learn?

What long-term and expansive relationships will I form?

What memorable experiences will I have?

A powerful source of guidance is the people who have done what you desire to do. Purposeful conversations with experienced individuals you respect—whether they are consultants, counselors, coaches, or mentors—will open your mind to see possibilities through new lenses. When a client is at this point in their lives, I suggest they request meetings with those who can help expand their knowledge of a course of action.

Who has done what you're considering?

Who asks the right questions at the right times?

Who sees this situation in ways I can't?

There are myriad ways to track and affirm your progress aligning with your curriculum. I've learned the most about myself and advanced the furthest by keeping a daily journal. It allows me to live in any moment fully and then later take notes about what I felt and learned. This continual feedback loop has moved me up the upward spiral of life curriculum more smoothly because I more rapidly see when the universe is softly presenting me with learning opportunities.

If you feel called to, buy and consistently use any popular journal you feel drawn to. There are many focused on expressing gratitude, and each page's questions and prompts will be helpful. For the last seven years, I've used a blank spreadsheet that I modified to offer me considerable space to type. It also allows me to search for keywords, and I can identify patterns. By noticing these patterns and comparing them to my mission, values, and goals, I'm able to implement habit changes for the next month.

You may also find value in keeping a "pain" journal. What I've asked clients to do is track any moment they felt a negative emotional trigger. After collecting these moments for two weeks, it's simpler to identify who caused the emotion, what occurred, and how specific feelings were brought to the surface. From there, you can make decisions about redistributing your time.

In a previous chapter, I mentioned how helpful The Pattern, World Numerology, and Co-Star apps have been. Each has a unique focus and way of helping you see your curriculum, but I find value in that each offers insight into how you'll feel. They can't tell you what will happen or how things will transpire, but they can guide you on the emotions you'll feel. That awareness and information are priceless in developing your emotional intelligence.

Addressing Emotions

I served on a board of directors for several years. One of the organization's employees, Crystal, attended many of the meetings and board events, but I didn't create opportunities to get to know her well. Five years after I termed off the board, a mutual friend invited us to a party. Right as I was about to leave, I saw Crystal out of the corner of my eye. We began talking, and the rest of the world turned off for me. Her life had just been turned upside down and she shared a traumatic event with me. Her husband had recently committed suicide. My heart sank and I instantaneously sensed I was meant to guide her to a new level of understanding. I also knew I'd learn something really important from her.

Although she was quite skeptical that the executive coach she knew five years previously could help her, she agreed to participate in my VIP Day. When we met, she shared that her father passed away when she was young. Without his presence, she used alcohol to deaden the pain of her reality. From age 13 until her late 20s, she used alcohol as a way to escape her emotions and curriculum. Instead of diving deep into each emotion, she chose to not feel the good or the bad deeply. She stayed on the surface, the same way I had done for decades. She got into a series of abusive romantic relationships, believing she could stay and fix them. Quickly, Crystal realized there was a correlation between escaping life by drinking alcohol and not being responsible for addressing her own emotions.

Through our dialogue, she realized her two ex-husbands chose not to be responsible for themselves. They chose not to take accountability for their actions and were using alcohol as an escape from their childhood traumas. When her third husband committed suicide, it was the awakener for Crystal because she has a son. She came to an agreement with herself that her son's well-being was more important than her desire to not release the emotions of her father's passing, the abusive relationships, and her husband's suicide. I have immense respect for Crystal and the strength she exuded through those events.

The universe brought her and me together in that room that evening to help her release the emotion around her husband's suicide (and me around my suicidal thoughts) but also to help her more deeply connect with her soul, her curriculum. It was empowering for Crystal to define her personal mission statement, to teach young people emotional well-being. She recognized her challenge—not releasing her emotions—and overcame it. She is now giving back to children who have similar circumstances she had. She wants to ensure they don't choose a life built around an alcohol addiction.

Today, Crystal volunteers with a local children's museum. She feels emotionally balanced. She can safely deep dive into her emotions and process them without taking them out on her body or others. She releases her anxieties through journaling, spending time in nature, and purposeful meetups with trusted friends.

The awakening and realignment to her Earth school curriculum have been completely life-changing. She finally allowed herself time to process emotions and connect the dots. She is supposed to experience deep vulnerable emotions, continually improve her emotional intelligence, and teach her son the power of learning and grieving childhood traumas and breaking unhealthy cycles.

Even though Avni is from India, Crystal is from Mexico, and I was raised in the United States, you may have noticed similarities in our stories. Our families didn't teach us to process our emotions. Our families taught us that emotions were better unaddressed. Our families taught us that what one family member does to another member should be allowed. Family members told Avni, Crystal, and I to stay in unloving relationships, to hide information, and to not experience emotions. We learned it was better not to talk about something even though openly expressing ourselves was the best thing we could have done.

We need to give children and teenagers permission and instruction on how to be expressive emotionally. The things that occurred in our formative years shape our habits, our choices, and who we become. If we are encouraged from a young age to trust and share our inner voices and express our feelings, we will have less difficulty to overcome later on in life.

Emotional Intelligence and Your Life's Mission

What does emotional intelligence (EQ) have to do with how we spend our time and live our missions? A lot, really. Growing your emotional intelligence helps you to know if you are ready to take action more aligned with who you actually are. It is also a powerful way to shed stale emotions or behaviors. EQ skills help you better manage your time in service of better living your life's mission. Emotional intelligence is defined by TTISI as "the ability to sense, understand and effectively apply the power of acumen of your emotions to facilitate higher levels of collaboration and productivity."[43]

For a person in the neutral zone, not knowing what to do next, clarity comes from reviewing the five components of EQ. I will do so here and discuss how I've grown my own emotional intelligence in each of these areas with the help of Aleah's influence. You're welcome to perform these alone or you can share with a group, a coach, or mentor to escalate your learning. The definitions of each component came from TTISI. Below each definition are activities you can perform to become stronger in that area of EQ.

1. Self-Awareness: The ability to recognize and understand your moods, emotions, and drives, as well as their effect on others.[44]

- As I discussed earlier in this chapter, track negative emotions in the pain journal or positive emotions in the gratitude journal to find connections between people, events, and your emotions.
- Proactively request feedback in the form of a professional 360-degree review, recommendations from colleagues or testimonials from clients, or via online personality assessment.

I looked myself in the mirror to understand how my decisions and parenting style negatively impacted Aleah. The way I worked to develop better self-awareness was to journal. What's happening emotionally for the people I love is a key source of information about how I'm progressing through my own curriculum. As I journaled, I released myself of the shame I felt for mistakes made. Feeling self-love was difficult when I started examining myself this way. But I'm glad I did it as it helped me open new conversations with Aleah.

Recently, now that Aleah is an adult, I could perform a parenting 360 and ask her directly: "What is it that I did when you were younger that was hurtful? Or that was limiting or stopped you?" She told me stories and gave examples of what she didn't like. She mentioned she didn't appreciate me trying to create rules about how she spent her time or how she completed her schoolwork. She didn't care about those things and thought they weren't important to her Earth school curriculum. The problem wasn't me asking her to do certain things; it was the repetition, the pattern of it being disconnected from her curriculum. As time passed, she lost trust in me. She shared less about her day and feelings. She felt I wasn't respecting her process of experiential learning.

Over a period of time, I began seeing myself and my purpose in her life differently. Seeing the patterns in my notes and directly receiving feedback from her was beyond enlightening. I shifted from the traditional Western role of parent to a more receptive stance of "This child is my teacher." By seeing how my emotions and habits affected her well-being and took her away from her curriculum, I learned a new level of self-awareness I now apply across all my relationships.

2. Self-Regulation: The ability to control or redirect disruptive impulses and moods and the propensity to suspend judgment and think before acting.[45]

- Openly share goals or intention publicly so trusted friends can provide in-the-moment, on-the-spot feedback to hold you accountable.
- Practicing calming breathing techniques, going for walks, and getting into nature weekly will limit the impulse to say or do hurtful things.

When I visited Aleah at school during her freshman year, we drove to her favorite camping spots. There was a calmness in sitting there talking about the good and the challenging, talking about our feelings and the things we wanted to do. If it wasn't for that time with her, I may not value nature, meditation, yoga, breathing techniques, or stillness the way I do today. I experienced how much more meaningful conversations could be when I wasn't moody or judgmental.

Aleah taught me the true value of those habits. I had read books about it, listened to podcasts about it, and made recommendations about it to others. But it was her and I together in nature—sitting there, experiencing it, and talking about it—that made me feel how to regulate my emotions. Don't get me wrong: I still feel emotionally triggered from time to time, but I can quickly regulate my reaction. I know how to control my fear and nervousness.

3. Motivation: A passion to work for reasons that go beyond external drives and are based on an internal drive or propensity to pursue goals with energy and persistence.[46]

- Defining your personal mission and wearing or looking at a physical reminder of that mission daily.
- Positive reinforcement, celebrating wins, and visualizing success keep you going even when you feel emotionally exhausted.

This is the capacity, even when the odds seem stacked against you, to keep moving toward a goal that matters to you. One of the ways I have helped people stay focused is to have them create visual reminders of their life's mission. To keep their mission top of mind, each person can have an item they see each day—whether a vision board on their bathroom mirror; something they carry in their pocket or purse; tattoos, clothing, jewelry, or artwork.

Two Christmases ago, Aleah bought me an I-Ching pendant that represented what she believed I needed more of in my experience the following year. I would hold the pendant in my hand and immediately feel connected to Aleah's guiding light. I wore the pendant on a chain almost every day that year.

4. Social Awareness: The ability to understand the emotional makeup of other people and how your words and actions affect others.[47]

- Work to become increasingly comfortable asking how, what, and why questions about others to uncover personal information.
- Paraphrase and validate back to a colleague what he or she said in your own words to ensure understanding.

This is the ability to recognize others' communication styles and adjust your communication to their preferences. Their emotions will likely be more balanced, and they'll feel empowered. I attempt to do this for Aleah by being an emotionally steady figure in her life. I desire to be reliable and trustworthy to her, but what she may need from me shifts. So I try to create safe environments where I can ask her questions to know how to adjust myself to her without losing what makes me, me.

Because Aleah and my relationships with our fathers are similar, when she experiences something difficult, I can validate her. I can confirm for her that what she's experiencing is real and I understand it because I've been—or helped a client—through something similar. In so many ways, these conversations have helped me heal my own father-related wounds. Plus, she can release anxiety around a circumstance, and I help her feel supported and loved. Being aware of the experiences of those who are close and how your words may affect them is deeply emotionally intelligent.

5. Social Regulation: The ability to influence the emotional clarity of others through a proficiency in managing relationships and building networks.[48]

- People can rely on you if you repeat the same action consistently.
- Establish recurring time blocks monthly to proactively reach out to and connect with key people.

I've found that clients do really well in deepening key relationships when they block their calendars at the same time each week for emotional connection with employees, vendors, and clients. By learning about and generating more value for others, the clients make those close to them feel appreciated. These feelings pay dividends later.

Social regulation is your ability to manage relationships over the long term. Once each month, I have a family dinner with Aleah, her mom, and her dad. Even though some would say it's unusual as I'm no longer in a romantic relationship with Aleah's mom, meeting for dinner fosters connection. This consistency gives me strength and makes each of us feel a part of something much bigger than ourselves. I think Aleah sees that no matter what, she has three parents who will consistently show up for her. She has people in her life that love her unconditionally that she can trust.

Respect Others' Journeys

A central tension in my work is that while I am encouraging you to proactively experience these processes and specific life-change steps, part of my message is also to learn how to relax and trust the universe's timing. Honestly, I've struggled with this: taking continuous action versus slowing down and being patient. When I started to slow down, to learn more about my emotions and curriculum from being still and less from repeating outdated habits, that's when I felt most connected to my life's mission.

When we think about developing our emotional intelligence, it's about recognizing that every person around us is also on their own version of a pain-to-purpose journey. Our role is to honor and respect their process. To not try to force the how of how we live our lives onto how they're living theirs. I am grateful to Aleah for helping me learn this lesson.

In 100 years, humanity will have ascended to a different and better place. I believe our souls chose to come to Earth during this interesting time in human evolution to do things that are emotionally hard. It's allowing our souls to ascend to a higher level of being more rapidly.

Key Takeaways

- We're all here to walk each other home.
- The true test of how aligned you are with your curriculum is where you invest your time.
- The deepest level of emotional intelligence is clearly recognizing that every single being on this planet is here to have experiences.

- It's okay to endure short-term pain to learn an important piece of your curriculum.
- If you spend an increasing percentage of your day living your mission and values, you will be engaged and happier.
- Pain journals are designed to identify who caused the emotion, what occurred, and how specific feelings came to the surface so you can make different choices in future situations.
- Life is not a one-tank journey. There will be several versions of you.
- The more emotionally intelligent you are, the more prepared you are for your life's next level.
- We can't stop ourselves from feeling emotions, but we can regulate our reactions to them.
- Block your calendar at the same time each week for a purposeful, proactive emotional connection with those around you.
- In the neutral zone, it's okay to accomplish less physically. Your focus is on shedding beliefs, people, and activities not suited for where you're headed.

Chapter 6: Shift Your Identity

"A person should not believe in an -ism, he should believe in himself. I quote John Lennon: 'I don't believe in Beatles, I just believe in me.' Good point there." ~Ferris Bueller's Day Off

As a second-year student at Thunderbird in 2009, I helped first-year students with resumes, LinkedIn profiles, cover letters, interview techniques, and job searches. This experience was so valuable to me that I shifted my career's focus away from general management to human resources and coaching. When I first started my coaching business in 2011, I wrote resumes. Then, I became an adjunct professor who taught entrepreneurship and human resources courses at Grand Canyon University (GCU). Because I was so naïve about the business of coaching, I had few clients and needed GCU's steady income. In 2013 and '14, I served as an Arizona State University employee who coached master's degree students in the W. P. Carey School of Business. I helped them with resumes, cover letters, interviews, and job searches. I helped SEED SPOT, a socially conscious startup incubator, write curriculum for their programs, and was named to the list 35 Entrepreneurs 35 and Younger by the Arizona Republic. I also self-published *Incorporate You.*

In 2015, I shifted into becoming a full-time small business owner who offered one-to-one communications coaching, team trainings, and public speaking. Working for anyone that would hire me, I had little focus as a coach in '15 or '16, but I did begin receiving recognition for my effort. I was named one of the Phoenix Business Journal's 40 Under 40, was invited to join class 38 of Valley Leadership,[49] and was voted onto the board of Big Brothers Big Sisters of Central Arizona. In 2017, I started speaking more about generational similarities. From there I moved into corporate strategy consulting and true executive coaching. In 2018, I spoke more about aligning personal branding, mission statements, and the core values that drive humans every day. The following year, I served clients as a staff psychologist, bringing conversations about authenticity into the workplace as well as offering the workshops and online courses.

As I reflect on how my coaching practice evolved, what I see more clearly is how my *identity* shifted. I moved from a lack of clarity about how I'd uplift others to strong belief about how my next steps would roll out in front of me. I moved from a place of limited confidence in my abilities to an unshakeable inner knowing that these processes can better millions of lives. I shifted from a corporate employee to a small business owner. I now only help people who seek my help when I used to help many for free.

Personally, I went from needing to be in a romantic relationship to being happy alone. I see patterns faster and act on them. I am far more patient with people as they awaken themselves; I don't try to awaken them faster. Instead, I manufacture learning experiences.

How has your own identity changed in the last 10 years? How will it change in the next 10? In this chapter, I invite you to shift your identity with intention. You are already fostering your inner knowing to do so. Now it's time to step into this new you.

Through small wins, begin to believe you can be, do, and achieve more.

Generational Similarities

No chapter about identity would be complete without acknowledging the generation you were born into. Does it mean something to you to say you are Generation X or a millennial?[50] Do you take care to set your identity as something apart from that of a generation born before yours? If so, that's okay, but I think it valuable to address that the generations alive today are actually much more alike than they are different.

In 2007, Jennifer J. Deal and the Center for Creative Leadership published *Retiring the Generation Gap*. Over seven years, she studied more than 3,000 leaders to find ways in which people from all generations are similar. Although each certainly has unique characteristics, humans have similar underlying motivations, needs, and values.[51] We want roughly the same things, but how we go about securing these things will be different because of what we were learning subconsciously from birth to age seven. Finding common ground shouldn't be as challenging as the media and society tell you it should be. Applying these principles may help you collaborate with, work for, attract, manage, retain, and develop leaders from all generations. In the subtlest ways, the media manipulates humans to focus on socio-economic differences instead of focusing on the ways all humans are fundamentally the same. Because conflict attracts more attention, news, the media, movies, and music often perpetuate a message of us-against-them that isn't entirely true and is the opposite of human nature.

It is useful to consider Carl Jung's four stages of human life here. Carl Jung, the Swiss psychiatrist and psychoanalyst who founded analytical psychology, created the Myers-Briggs Type Indicator and wrote extensively on the topic of human transitions. According to him, the four stages of human life are not focused on age or accomplishment but rather on our values and what motivates us to take action.[52]

In phase one, the athlete, we're self-absorbed and focused on how our physical body looks. In phase two, the warrior, we find ways to display our authentic self, set and achieve big goals, and focus on material gain. In phase three, the statement, we learn the world is much bigger than self-interest and material possessions, and we begin working to make the world a better place. Finally, in stage four, the spirit, we realize that we're simply souls having a human experience. Most humans don't reach stage four.

The phase of life a person is in will likely be a bigger predictor of outward behavior than the generation he or she was born into. As Jung put it very eloquently, "I am not what happened to me, I am what I choose to become." The exiting generation, as they are passing power, is quick to say the following generation is lazy, entitled, or selfish. A quick review of popular media from the last century, and you'll see this happens over and over regardless of the generation in power. Baby boomers were once called out by the traditionalists for protesting the Vietnam War and experimenting with cannabis. Then we saw baby boomers calling out Gen X for being "slackers," and members of Gen Y for being "snowflakes," and on and on.

In my experience, when generational conflict occurs, we are seeing disagreement about when, how, and why someone moves between life stages. Movement happens at different ages for each generation. Boomers did some things earlier in life such as getting married, buying homes, or having children in their 20s. Because of technology, the internet, and globalization, members of Generation Y have chosen to do those same things in their early 30s. People are learning to focus less on the things that are dissimilar between generations and more on the environmental factors that forced the changes in decisions and moving between stages. This may help people from different generations feel empathy and greater connection.

Look at someone quite different than you in terms of gender, age, skin color, or income and realize that individual is on Earth to complete their Earth school curriculum, too. Don't compete against that person. Think about how you can help them. See yourself in them. Seek areas of commonality with one another before addressing differences in life experience and what each has learned. Get curious about what others were taught from birth to age seven and how that impacted them throughout life.

Each generation is encouraged to blame the one before it for society's ills. Thankfully, it's our time to be more emotionally intelligent, to honor another's curriculum, to see the oneness of all humans.

Create . . . Yourself

I interviewed Anthony Trucks for my podcast *Equal Chance to Be Unequal*. Anthony played in the NFL and was a contestant on *American Ninja Warrior* before transitioning into speaking, consulting, and coaching. Despite significant early life challenges, including a variety of emotional traumas, Anthony has built a beautiful business and family life. He created his identity by believing the future could be better than the past. I honor him for this, and I am glad people worldwide are being inspired by his message.

As you've released old emotions, defined your guiding statements, and improved your emotional intelligence, it's easy to feel lost. Please know you are not. Your authentic self is buried deep within you, under socio-cultural conditioning, under something a parent wished for you to have, or beneath some inaccurate conclusion you drew as a child about the world. Finding your true identity is a process of returning to yourself, shedding untrue beliefs you picked up over time, getting back to the basics of your curriculum.

So how do we move back toward who we were before the world conditioned us to believe something different? Believe it is okay to walk into your true, authentic identity. It is okay to have everything you desire. It is okay to shed pieces of yourself and move into the amazing human and soul you are. To illustrate this process, let's imagine you want to convince yourself you have already received a work promotion to a prominent leadership role. Your new identity will be that of a person who is comfortable influencing teams to achieve important organizational goals.

Here is the process:

1. Begin by asking, "What evidence do I have I might already be considered a leader?" Are there action-oriented things leaders in your company do that you also do? Do you read the same books? Engage in similar daily habits? Develop others' talents naturally? Help your colleagues feel happy and engaged at work? Received supportive LinkedIn recommendations? See how the organization's strategy will play out in the marketplace?

My guess is you've been doing many of the things—for years—that are evidence you *are* a leader. Right now. Make a list of as many examples as possible. Talk to colleagues for additional examples you may have forgotten.

Look for signs of certainty around you. What wins have you had that point to this identity? Prove to yourself you are already what you desire to be. The only difference between you and another person who is currently a leader is time. They may have been in the role for a period of time, but their signs of certainty are nearly identical to yours.

What examples do you have leading others? When did you make something innovative happen? When did you bring a project to completion ahead of a deadline? When did you receive recognition from mentors? Have you stuck to a set of habits that serve you well? Have you learned new skills ahead of going after this promotion?

2. Figure out: "What is the story I am telling myself about the new identity I'd like to adopt?" Think about the emotional reasons you would like to move into this leadership role. What would it mean to you? Why? How does it help you live your life's mission more fully? Would it benefit your family? Would it heal childhood emotional traumas? Detail reasons and a good story about why this new identity matters to you and how it helps you move closer to or stay on your curriculum.

3. Ask, "How can I use fear as a motivator?" What may happen if I don't take action toward this new identity? Perhaps your organization frowns on not progressing via regular role changes. Staying in one place could be seen as falling behind. A colleague may get the promotion. You won't earn the higher salary that will help you afford to send your child to a specific university. Maybe you won't be able to go on the vacation you'd hoped to. Maybe you'll move further from your curriculum, and trying to reconnect with it later will be more painful. Make this list of potential consequences that could occur if you stayed stuck in an old identity. I can't tell you how many clients I've served who talked about their life regrets and what they wished they would've taken calculated risks on. Now they can't.

4. Shed old beliefs. When moving toward a new identity, we set goals and invest time into important actions to prove we are worthy of our goal. Sometimes you may have to release emotions connected to your old identity to make room for the new to enter. For me, there are two yoga poses that make me cry uncontrollably. I struggle to release emotions connected to who I was. When I feel that need to release, investing an hour into a yoga flow helps me clear space for a new way of being to arrive. Other activities that may be helpful here include walks, meditation, journaling, and cold showers.

5. Reward yourself. We benefit immensely when we receive continual praise and recognition for a job well done. When you commit to a growth plan, unexpected emotions are likely, and you'll stay motivated as you set goals and reward yourself each step of the way to your new identity. What reward would be meaningful to you? Perhaps it's a long weekend spent with friends. Maybe it's a regular spa appointment, tee time, or a hike. Whatever it is, block your calendar and make space for it in your life. Celebrate your milestones along the way.

All humans have a curriculum of lessons to learn and emotions to experience. And then our parents, cultural conditioning, and the education system shift our focus away from that learning. Our job is to get back to who we were before age seven. Shed the beliefs that aren't serving you so you can live in the now—and love what it is you are doing and who you are becoming. This is worthwhile for you to do on a personal level, but undergoing these changes is also hugely beneficial for society at large.

Getting Back to Fundamentals

In some cases, ascending to your next identity involves returning to a part of yourself that you've left behind. It's like asking what you wanted to be when you were young to find out what you might want to do professionally now. This happened to my client Luke. Along his journey, he had lost a key piece of himself, and it was affecting many pieces of his life. When he reconnected with that forgotten part of himself, the pieces started to fall into place again.

As a young adult, Luke was searching for something he couldn't find. He jumped from university to community college to university. He traveled to different places globally. Eventually, he found a sense of belonging, identity, and family when he joined a fraternity. He felt clarity, and his identity began to be shaped by physical fitness and competitive sport. He loved to play sports with his brothers. He was really active, playing volleyball and other team sports. Luke's identity was born out of being able to control his body and to make it look and perform a certain way.

As he got into a career post-college, Luke gained weight. His focus shifted from physical fitness to growing and selling several businesses. When he called me, the one business he was focused on was stagnant and he was 50-pounds heavier than he desired to be. There seemed to be an ethereal connection between his body feeling out of sorts and his business being out of sorts. We began a six-month process of improving his physical and emotional well-being. It was powerful for him to reflect on his college years and recreate those feelings of success and connection. When Luke stopped dealing with his emotions at a surface level, his fortunes shifted.

He realized that he needed to experiment with both his body *and* his business—to take calculated risks he hadn't before. In the three years since we invested in one another, Luke reimagined his business. Once he got to that level of depth for himself emotionally, the lightbulb turned on and he realized there was a new and untapped market he needed to address. By reconnecting to a previous positive identity, Luke was able to find unique ways to recreate those fundamental feelings and move closer to his curriculum.

An Organization-Wide Identity Shift

Can one person change an entire organization's identity? Yes. An organization's identity is its culture and it's *everything*. Fortunately, leaders are recognizing the importance of culture and are investing resources to improve it, for the good of every employee and society at large.

In 2018, I was engaged by the leadership of a consulting firm with 325 employees. The firm had recently changed CEOs and was determining what culture it wanted to create to uplift employees so they could best serve clients. Under the previous leader, the culture could have been described as command and control. Employees had been trained to act according to a leader's request or directive. Few were willing to take risks or follow their intuition. I started my work having one-to-one conversations with employees from each level of the organization. Repeatedly, they said things like "I don't deserve that promotion," "I'm not ready for this role," "I don't know if I can talk to this client," and, the one that hurt my heart most, *"I don't know."*

No one person was at fault, but over time, a culture of employees limiting themselves and waiting for someone else to make decisions became prevalent. The safest way to keep your job was to deflect decision-making responsibility up the corporate ladder. Also, many on the team were task-oriented introverts who enjoyed receiving direction from a leader. They enjoyed completing projects. They liked linear processes and a harmonious workplace. They found value in the familial feeling the office provided. Our work was to gently move the employees from waiting for directions from a leader to empowerment where they trusted their intuition, shared their expertise more, and uplifted one another. This was an important identity shift needed to make their long-term strategy viable. We couldn't do it overnight. Each employee needed to play a role in shaping the culture the firm would become.

As I spoke with leadership, we encouraged the use of a number of tools to help them empower their employees. One tool we used to open new dialogue was when an employee sought direction from a leader, we asked the leader to not offer solutions. We encouraged them to ask how, what, and why questions that would pull three possible solutions out of the employee.

At that point, the leader then offered support for a course of action that aligned with the department's goals. As employees talked more about possible solutions, they started feeling safe that their ideas were good. They felt comfortable taking more responsibility. They saw how their decisions were contributing to the firm's success. They were slowly realizing that they had the answers inside of them.

As the organization's culture shifted, the CEO invited me to train 35 of its employees. Over a two-day training, we talked about many of the processes you're reading about in this book. These employees became internal coaches who empowered themselves and every team member to proactively shift their and the firm's identity.

They've had thousands of internal coaching conversations using the process I described earlier in this chapter. Not only did exploring the answers release a limiting belief on the part of each employee, but it also nudged the employee into seeing themself as being far more advanced, far smarter, far more capable than what they may have ever felt themself to be. It was a grassroots, and extremely powerful, way for this organization to shift its culture and achieve bigger goals.

Of course, the firm still has pockets of employees who complete tasks the old way. Change is uncomfortable. Thankfully, most employees feel safe to take control of their careers, to be proactive, to seek new learning, and to contribute to their community. The old ethos of waiting for a leader to provide an answer and course of action has been replaced by purposely created cross-functional teams who are committed to solving challenges together and for one another.

The decentralization of decision-making has been so helpful. It's taken power from the status quo, the way things were in the Age of Pisces. The firm is moving decision-making authority to *every* employee—into the Age of Aquarius. This allows the organization's board and CEO to be acutely focused on strategy. This organization doesn't simply have 325 employees. They now have 325 people who are culture ambassadors and recruiters talking about how much they enjoy working there. All employees have become sales people with the tools, ideas, and resources needed to share the diverse services the firm offers.

As a result of this empowerment, the firm has weathered coronavirus relatively unscathed. They maintained their staffing levels. They bettered their client relationships. In a matter of weeks, they launched new services. According to Dr. Judith A. Howard at the University of Washington, in her review of the social-psychological underpinnings of identity, as humans, our identities are born out of the groups we belong to.[53] Because the employees at the consulting firm have gone through this process of coming up with more solutions and being able to deal with challenges on their own, they're now able to contribute and have their opinions be heard in a way they weren't even a year ago. And they genuinely feel great to be a part of the team. Employee engagement scores are up. There are virtual happy hours, book clubs, a Netflix club, retirement celebrations, and more. Their identities have grown through feeling proud to work with this firm.

Climb Over Your Identity Wall

Anthony Trucks spoke about the concept of an "identity wall" in our podcast. When someone is running into a wall—they can't yet see themself as that next thing, getting a promotion or finishing that marathon—how can they get past it? It's not easy. You might be facing an identity wall yourself.

The key is to take the next step, however small. Be willing to get uncomfortable. Try something new, no matter how seemingly insignificant it appears to be. If you're willing to take a minor calculated risk, the probability of you being able to eventually see yourself as that new thing is much higher. You might surprise yourself. You may just realize you actually are that new identity, and that small step may be the thing that helps you prove it to yourself.

This happened to me recently with how I identify as a golfer.

Some of my happiest moments occurred on golf courses. When I was young and pretty good at the game, I felt a deep level of confidence. Now that my golf game is improving again at age 40, it's no coincidence I'm feeling more confident in life in general. There's an ethereal connection there—the same way Luke experienced. When we remember those pieces of our lives when we were really happy, productive, or clear, that's when we feel confident. As we experience life's cycles, returning to an earlier habit or mindset can be uplifting.

When my ex-wife left in 2008, I started the MBA and disconnected from the things that used to make me feel like I belonged. From 2008 through 2019, I didn't play much golf, maybe once per month. That seemed to be enough for me as my curriculum shifted and I was learning much from the professional circles I was a part of.

I now have profound clarity about my curriculum, who my soul is, and where I should invest time. My brand as a speaker, coach, and consultant is solidified and growing. The improvement in my golf game happens to be a good metaphor for the confidence I feel. Playing today teaches me new levels of self-awareness that I quickly apply to other areas of my life.

In March 2020, I set the goal to have a 3 handicap. A handicap is a numerical measure of a golfer's potential—what they're capable of shooting in relation to a course's par. When I achieved the goal, I agreed to buy myself a new set of clubs. As of August, I reached the goal. In September, I was fitted for and received the new clubs in October. I enjoyed such a deep feeling of accomplishment by achieving my goal and following through with my plan to reward myself for doing so.

My identity as a golfer has shifted, and I can now say I've ascended to a new level. The progress is a direct result of intentional effort. I set a goal. I trusted the process. I experimented. I made time for reflection. I watched videos of myself. I tracked important metrics each round. I shed old swing thoughts and habits. I introduced new routines and areas of focus. The same thing happens with a person who's developing a new identity. Luke tried different approaches with his body and his businesses. He experimented, collected data, and surrounded himself with new people that helped him ascend to his next level.

And I'm doing the same. It wasn't just about the process of getting better at golf. It was about changing my identity.

A Deeper Level of Healing Awaits

Identity is born out of groups you're a part of and out of the unique attributes that distinguish you. My intuition guides me to believe we're moving to a society where we identify less with the former and far more with the latter. Identity is often produced through self-talk. If you repeatedly speak your mission, values, and goals, you'll align with your curriculum more easily. Identity struggles are often born out of pain. When we convert what brought us pain into a learning opportunity, we move closer to our life's purpose. The struggle (or, according to Buddhists, the suffering) is a core component of our authentic identity. A whole, authentic person will shift identities as they climb the upward spiral.

You now have a better understanding of the discovery portion of your *I Know* journey. This takes time and wins to integrate as we need others to confirm our beliefs and we need to accomplish goals to believe we are at our life's next level. You'll know you are there when you no longer feel triggered emotionally by things that used to trigger you. You'll spend less time with old friends and more time with new friends. Your verbiage adjusts. You'll no longer say you "hope to be . . ."; you'll say "I am . . ."

You will stop serving organizations that aren't connected to your mission. You will say "no" more. You begin to feel clearer about the future as you slow down and trust the process more. You stop blaming others for your problems.

You are ready to help others awaken. There's a completely new level waiting for you once you start teaching these concepts to others. An incredibly deep level of healing occurs when you help others who have gone through something similar to what you've gone through. It's hard to fathom right now, but trust me: it'll happen for you, and you'll love it.

Remember, the pain-to-purpose journey says you 1) went through pain and 2) overcame it. Now 3) you will help other people overcome it. It's your chance to contribute to something bigger than yourself, to unlock another person or group's potential. You are ready.

Have the courage to go out and put to work the stuff you've learned in this section of the book. Test it. Be okay with whatever comes back. Identify patterns. Adjust. Reflect. Repeat. You've done tremendous work getting through this neutral zone of learning. Now you're going into a phase where the impact from your learning will benefit others and you'll heal more deeply.

In this second part of the *I Know* journey, you've done three very challenging things: you've taken the time to identify your core values, motivators, and life's mission. You've considered your emotional intelligence and ways to grow it while finding the ways, big and small, to use your time more wisely. Finally, you've learned how to shift and up-level your identity.

You are ready for the third and final part of this process: to share exactly who you are and begin to help others as an authentic leader. Let's go!

Key Takeaways

- In order for your life to evolve, your identity must evolve first.
- Change is uncomfortable.

- Trying and struggling appears to be incompetence right up until the moment it looks like success.
- See those around you as a mirror for your own journey.
- Control less. Get in flow more. Trust yourself more.
- Seek new experiences purely to experience more learning, feeling, and memory.
- Although each generation has unique characteristics, they're far more similar than dissimilar.
- Environmental factors are an important contributor to how each generation moves between Jung's four life stages.
- Returning to your identity is a process of shedding untrue beliefs you picked up over time.
- Reconnecting with a previous successful version of yourself can bring clarity to your life's next steps.
- Empowerment is often born out of asking the right how, what, and why questions.
- Cross-functional teams distribute empowerment and decision-making throughout an organization.
- The key to overcoming an identity wall is to take the next step, no matter how small.
- Experiment. Collect data. Iterate. Repeat.
- Your pain is your purpose. Your mess is your message.

Part Three

Decision

Share your new brand with the world, engage and lead more deeply engaged teams, and create an entire organization of employees coaching themselves and each other.

Description: new beginnings, searching for solutions

Actions You're Taking: Finding ways to help others. Showing empathy and listening actively. Living in the NOW, trusting the process. Showing gratitude and appreciation. Living your life's mission. Adapting to change willingly. Living happily and sharing hope.

Challenges You're Encountering: Finding the right new opportunities. Getting enthusiastic about possibility. Maintaining openness to learning and action.

Your Focus: Us: "I'm part of the team—let's go!"

Ask Yourself: What progress have I made? Who can I show gratitude to? Who can I lift up and help? How do I stay committed to my plan? Who can I energize?

To Find Balance, You'll Be Influenced By: compelling vision, stories, celebrations

What You Can Communicate to Uplift Others: *Clearly show examples of "why." Show how all can contribute. Celebrate wins weekly. Recognize why changes were made. Have the team share excitement.*

Chapter 7: Share Your Brand

Imagine that the world had no middlemen, no publishers, no bosses, no HR folks, no one telling you what you couldn't do. If you lived in that world, what would you do? Go do that. ~Seth Godin

Are you getting excited about the person you've discovered inside? You've given your inner voice—and inner wisdom—the chance to be heard. And it turns out she's very talkative.

Are you ready to share your true energy with the world?

I believe you are. If you've reached this final part of the book, you are done hiding.

Living in alignment with our curriculum and openly sharing our value proposition, or brand, allows us to be in flow, to trust, to release expectation, to stop trying to control others, to learn from and add value to everything and everyone we meet. Living out of alignment with our curriculum, mission, and brand creates unnecessary feelings of lack, shame, and fear. We don't behave in an emotionally intelligent way and are likely to treat others poorly.

I admire author and marketing guru Seth Godin as he's very clear on who he is and how he wants to add value to society.

He's written a number of books about the methods we can use to change marketing and professional culture as society evolves. Probably 10 years ago, I read his book *Linchpin*, and it was a transformative experience for me. He talked about the unique characteristics that are you—how authentic you are, the things you can do to best share yourself in the marketplace.

He helped me explore parts of myself I hadn't considered before. I started to believe in new ways I could be a linchpin for a community of people, an organization, or a nonprofit. It made me think differently about how I could share unique stories about my journey. What to say about my character traits, strengths, and skills that may help me be better understood by those around me. I hadn't seen the world through those lenses prior to reading *Linchpin*. It was a new level of awareness for me when I began leaving behind a no-longer-needed version of myself and thought more intentionally about my legacy. How was I really going to help society?

What Living in "Decision" and Sharing My Authenticity Feels Like to Me

I feel closely aligned with my Earth school curriculum today. I'm patient. I've learned to see mundane life moments as important to the journey as the accomplishments that society celebrates. I proactively choose activities simply for the learning opportunity I would gain from the experience. I accept that my soul's emotional growth is infinitely more valuable than any Earthly accomplishment.

I control my emotional reactions almost immediately. I'm deeply proud of my website and the resources it offers. I can push my body harder and further than I ever have before. In the gym, I lift heavier weights. I run further on hiking trails. I'm grateful for my relationship with Tiffany. If you are reaching a similar place in your Earth school curriculum, you might find yourself enjoying a greater sense of satisfaction while completing work projects, more peace or understanding in your family relationships, or better sleep.

A Day in the Life

One of the best ways to share your brand and live fully into your Earth school curriculum is to set up daily habits that serve your highest good. I help clients design lives that allow for more of what energizes and inspires them. This starts with me modeling my version of that behavior in my own day. I sleep between six to eight hours each night and wake up between 4:30 a.m. and 5 a.m.

Cleopatra likes to be served her food early, so I care for her and then go into the spare bedroom and sit in the lotus position. I meditate for 20 minutes. I use the Insight Timer app[54] for soothing sounds and as an alarm to know when to exit the meditation. As the years have passed, my meditations have looked different. I've repeated "I am" statements. I've repeated my guiding statements. I've followed guided meditations. I've sat in silence allowing any messaging to come through. I've visualized what I hope will happen that day. I've asked questions about a dream I had the night before or something I struggled with the day before. This start to the day gives me balance. I sit there with no expectations. I'm simply being and in flow with my curriculum.

Cleo and I go outside. I sit while she explores the yard. I check email. I review my astrology reports from The Pattern, World Numerology, and Co-Star. I think through the impact of what the reports suggest for the day. I structure the day to live peacefully and continue learning my curriculum. Then I exercise. Preferably at an instructor-led class. Sometimes a trail run. Sometimes yoga. Regardless, I give 100% of my focus and energy.

When I've returned home, I prepare a vegan protein smoothie and take vitamins and supplements. Getting the right nutrients that oxygenate and create an alkaline blood pH has helped me in so many ways.

Each morning, I try to complete my most challenging work project first. I find myself continually asking, What's Important Now? The WIN acronym has helped me focus and be more productive. If possible, I get my most difficult task done before 9:00 a.m. or 10:00 a.m. as my mind is acute and highly functioning. It makes me feel as though I've really accomplished something. I'll have phone calls with clients throughout the day. My work often involves being available, last minute, for whatever a client may need. I have more structure in the morning and less in the afternoon purposely. Given the unexpected nature of who I serve and how I help them, flexibility benefits all involved.

Once it gets closer to 6:00 p.m., Tiffany is finishing her workday. We have time for connection. She is a tremendous cook and loves to create. It's a release for her. Many nights, she'll create a meal for us to share. As she's preparing dinner, I am in the kitchen and we catch up about our days' events. When the meal is ready, we share a champagne toast and enjoy the food and one another's company. It's important to me Tiffany feels equity in our relationship, so I clean the dishes and kitchen.

As the day comes to a close, I wind down. I'll read a book on my phone or watch a short documentary. It helps me integrate the day's learning. I may read a handful of news sources or scroll my favorite social media accounts to feel inspired. All of a sudden, it's 9:30 p.m. and we're ready for bed.

Sometimes it's hard to stick to this intentional way of life. When I was young, I was subconsciously taught that I had to act and achieve to be loved, accepted, and successful. Fortunately, I've learned I'm good enough just the way that I am, without any action. I have peace now. That's a sizable transformation from who I was when I was younger. I enjoy being present and sending good vibes out into the universe to heal people.

Consistently Sharing Your Message

With a defined mission statement, core values, and goals, you can become more intentional about the daily habits associated with your online presence—and how it looks and feels to others. For some clients, I help them identify a color that represents the feeling they want others to associate with who they are. Different colors have unique subconscious meanings to humans. To learn more about this, I recommend Sally Hogshead's book *How to Fascinate*. Sally teaches the meanings of each primary color and how you can use those meanings to best display your authentic brand.

I've also offered suggestions about the color of a client's clothing, the colors of the background on their social media profiles or the pictures they share on their websites. By identifying the colors that best help them explain their brand, it's an easy way for people to share who they are socially.

Next, I invite you to consider how you can consistently use the same themes, patterns, or values repeatedly. Robert Cialdini's Law of Consistency states that by doing so, after a reasonable period of time, people will start to subconsciously know you.[55] Some people are creative and they share their authentic message through music, art, or theatrical performance. Some people are like me: they're quieter and use the written word. How you share your brand with the world is up to you. Being consistent in the delivery of that message is the important thing, so people can really come to know you.

You are living your curriculum when you feel in flow, have released expectations, and are learning from and adding value to everyone you meet.

Designing Your Time

The average American only productively works 2 hours and 53 minutes each day.[56] If we don't have the right goals and time management frameworks inside the workplace, it's easy for an organization to get off track and miss its most important goals. If we don't openly share our brand with our communities, we're likely to become overinvolved with activities disconnected from our curriculum.

When I speak to audiences, how humans make decisions keeps coming back as one of the most important parts of my content. One of my clients has struggled mightily with controlling her time. She's a principal at an accounting firm and has said yes to most of the requests made of her. This approach has limited her greatly. She feels unhealthy and stressed. As a single mother, she wants more time with her young son. It took her three years longer than it could have to get promoted. She openly admits to not sharing her brand or her goals. She didn't make time to train or delegate tasks to her team.

A big part of managing your time is simply handling unwelcome demands and bids for your attention. According to the *International Journal of Work and Stress*, there are 85 interruptions during the workday.[57] Interruptions can come from seemingly limitless sources, including family, colleagues, clients, technology, the environment, and more. It's no wonder that in 2018, according to Gallup, 55% of Americans experienced stress "a lot of the day," 45% felt worried, and 22% felt anger.[58] A lack of clarity around your time leads to a feeling of not being able to meet all the needs people have for you.

People who are crystal clear about where they need to devote their time don't get interrupted as much. Open-door policies can be effective at building camaraderie, but the trade-off is you'll be far less productive. There's value in surrounding yourself with emotionally intelligent people who help you know what activities actually produce results.

Jim Rohn famously said, "The best-kept secret of the rich is not genius or brilliance—it's the management of time."

When You Face Pushback From Old Belief Systems

As you begin sharing your brand and story with society, expect to encounter resistance. Balancing our own inner wisdom with outside input and outside opinions can be challenging. So when you do encounter older ways of thinking, I want to offer you ideas for handling it. One strategy is to ask the universe for a sign you are on the right path. At dinner recently, a friend and I talked about this as he is considering options for a major career decision.

What we came to, through considering a plethora of different decision-making criteria, was that he wanted an agreed-upon sign from the universe. It would give him additional confidence that his choice was being divinely inspired. That could manifest as a ladybug on his next hike, a hummingbird in his backyard, or hearing from a friend he hadn't talked with in a while. Another idea is to talk through your decision with 10 different people. Invest 30 days to gather opinions and information to see if a pattern emerges toward one course of action.

A third idea is to ask specific questions while in meditation. If the messaging you continue getting back, day after day, is that you should go down one path, trust the message you're receiving and act on it.

In the Age of Pisces, 7.8 billion people were convinced through social conditioning that we should admire and emulate celebrities, athletes, and politicians. As society continues its shift into the Age of Aquarius and more people stop believing in others' paths, there will be those who enjoyed and felt safest in the old mindset. If you're ready for the age of knowing and believe wholeheartedly in your authentic path, good for you. Keep going.

When you interact with those who want you to return to what they perceive as the right way of life, say and do nothing. Instead of offering a response, judging, pushing back, and responding emotionally . . . do nothing. Allow them the dignity of their process and to learn their Earth school curriculum in their time. In my experience, the people who try to pull you back to their level live in fear. They fear how their life will change. Because they're disconnected from their own path, they may not have the capability to honor your progress on yours.

When this occurs, look within. All persons we interact with are a mirror for our learning. If someone else is behaving in a way that is emotionally triggering for you, get quiet and write responses to the following.

What is the universe teaching me through this person?

When have I done something nearly identical to someone else?

How can I release my stale emotions so this situation doesn't repeat itself?

How can I apologize to myself for what happened?

I see these situations as being about forgiveness. When you are continually confronted by a similar emotion, take a step back and see that others are responding in the way they were taught to. By looking at the situation objectively and removing your desire to blame others for your learning, you take your power back.

I'm clear with clients at this stage of awakening: only share the pieces of your journey the individual can actually comprehend. Meet people where they are. By doing this, you aren't judging or saying someone isn't at your level. Instead, in a positive and loving way, you're showing up for that person in a way they can receive and be inspired by your journey. Only sharing the parts of your story that they can understand shows growth on your behalf. Trying to impress them with your knowledge or trying to get them to change is unlikely to work. Words don't teach. Experiences do. As you continue to lead by example, they may later approach you and ask how they can feel the same way you do. At that point, and that point only, will they be open for a vulnerable discussion about the processes in this book. Share your journey authentically with people who genuinely want to learn more. Help the people who ask for it.

In the early 2000s, my family's business experienced steady growth. My dad invested in a new building, only to have the economic crisis hit in '08. Over the next year, customers didn't renew contracts, employees left, revenue dipped, and my parents chose to sell their second home in Tucson. I can't imagine the stress my dad must have felt. It seemed like he lived in constant sadness. Seeing that really bothered me at the time, but part of my curriculum was learning that no matter how I offered to help, he wasn't ready to receive it. Every suggestion I offered fell on deaf ears. It was hard, but I needed to experience that. I slowly stopped helping and chose to honor that he'd learn his curriculum in the time right for him, not in the time right for me.

You can try anything in the world and think you're helping, but more likely than not, it's not going to facilitate change if the person doesn't want advice. You may make the problem worse by trying to project your experiences and what you believe to be the right path onto that person. You're better off to truly understand your journey and that others may not desire to walk that path alongside you. Simply honor their journey. Communicate to them in a way that they can really feel heard.

Now, when family members do things I wouldn't do, I don't offer judgment. I realize I don't have their information. When I begin to feel the desire to judge someone because they're not taking my advice or not using resources I suggested, I fully release my emotion and say quietly to myself, "I have not been there for their life each day. I don't know their childhood traumas. I don't understand why they're doing what they're doing. Why would I want to force them to change?"

Seeing others' progress on their curriculum through that lens has changed my life. It offers you peace. It offers them peace. It's a gift both ways. You are aligned with your Earth school curriculum when what used to trigger you no longer does.

Why You Must Share Your Story

When you are joining a new organization or a new team, and you don't set expectations with your new leader, or don't take the time to share more about who you are, problems will likely arise. You can stack the deck in your favor if you set expectations at the beginning of the relationship with a new leader. Of course, you may encounter a situation in which a boss is not receptive to your story or ideas. In this case, you need to redirect the conversation when he or she doesn't respond favorably. Regardless of the immediate response you get, there is value in presenting how you know yourself and giving your boss this information. Truth-telling is healthy and makes an impression on a boss. Thus, we should be unafraid to share. While not every boss will handle it well, this gives us an opportunity to practice being okay in a variety of circumstances.

I believe there's power in narrative. Sharing our life stories with our bosses creates deeper levels of empathy. This will open communication, establish trust, and make conflict resolution simpler. Unemotional relationships based on transactional communication are disconnected, unproductive, and underperforming. If we're not appreciating ourselves for who we are and we're not sharing our journey with the people we work with, we're going to be disengaged.

If you are beginning a new job, starting with a new team, or picking up a new project, here are ways you can set expectations clearly and begin building a strong relationship with your leader:

1. **Explain three to five ways you enjoy being communicated to.** Using the DISC report, what may trigger your fear? What is your negotiation style? Under stress, what is your default emotion? What makes you feel validated and heard? What is harmful to you in dialogue?
2. **Share what motivates you.** From the 12 Driving Forces report, what are your top motivators? How would you like to live them at work? In what ways are your job description's tasks and responsibilities motivating to you?
3. **Share your strengths, skills, and talents.** Using the Authority section in chapter 4, talk with your new leader about ways you can spend an increasing percentage of your day completing tasks that use your strengths.
4. **Let your boss know what they can say when you veer off track.** Talk through how you'd like them to communicate with you when you are visibly off, not meeting deadlines, or not accomplishing goals. What can

your boss say to make you feel supported? What can they do to help you learn from a mistake?

5. **Communicate how you like to receive appreciation.** The Languages of Appreciation assessment is helpful.[59] Ask your leader to recognize you in the way you prefer when you accomplish goals.

6. **Share your short- and long-term goals.** Whatever your personal, professional, or relationship goals may be, your leader can then help open serendipitous doors. They can also serve as an accountability partner and keep you motivated.

7. **Share your personal mission.** If your boss knows your purpose, they can connect the organization's mission and values to your personal mission and core values. You'll feel a stronger connection, more engaged, and a part of something bigger than yourself.

8. **Communicate the type of organizational culture you thrive in.** If there's a way your boss can help to create that around you, it's engaging. When a flower is not blossoming, you don't fix the flower. You fix the environment in which it grows. You give it more sun, or more water, or new soil. You'll feel more engaged if the company culture is a fit for your preferences.

The theme here is the importance of attaining self-knowledge to design a personal brand and then parlaying that brand and narrative intentionally. Sharing the items above requires trust. You may have to be the first and initiate openly sharing your story and preferences. The quality of the relationship you build with your boss is a determinant of happiness in your career.

Are You Seeing the Possibilities?

I believe we can all be a *possibility-tarians*. We can create possibilities and meaningful moments for the people we work with. A big part of sharing your story and personal brand is creating experiences that evoke emotions in the people around you. They'll always remember how you made them feel.

In the 1970s, '80s, and '90s, large organizations were known for being strict, for having excessive rules, for not allowing mistakes. Society has rapidly transitioned to a place where we've focused more on empowering our workforce, connecting them, and equipping them with the right tools. This transition requires more in-depth, transparent and authentic dialogues. Leaders should be constantly communicating their philosophies. We have to "manage up" to those philosophies, and the only way to do that is to continuously share them and lead by example.

Communicate your personal brand by doing some or all of the following items:

- Launch a new resume.
- Improve your LinkedIn profile.
- Write a new biography or build websites.
- Tweak your online persona.
- Choose a signature color.

The more we proactively communicate our message, and the more we proactively help one another, the faster an organization grows. As a result, the organization will be more profitable and successful, because a group of people can always accomplish more together than they can separately.

Key Takeaways

- Shed the old belief structure of who you "are."
- Realign use of time to accomplish more.
- Form new healthier daily or weekly habits.
- Stop doing things that bring you pain.
- It's okay to choose experiences simply for what you'll learn from them.
- A fulfilling life is full of daily habits that serve you.
- Each day, multiple times, ask yourself, "What's Important Now?"
- Color has deep subconscious meaning; align your social profiles, websites, clothing, etc., with the color that best represents your brand.
- How you share your brand is less important than how consistently you share it.
- Make sure a "yes" to someone else is not a "no" to yourself.
- Allow others the dignity of their process.
- Blaming others for your life's challenges is a sign you're out of alignment with your curriculum.
- Meet people where they are.
- Communicate to others in a way they feel heard, understood, and loved.

Chapter 8: Lead an Engaged Team

Everything that irritates us about others can lead us to an understanding of ourselves. ~Carl Jung

Hope was a talented administrative assistant to the CEO at a technology organization I consulted. Members of the C-suite began to realize that Hope was quite capable of leading a larger team. She exuded the organization's core values and was in tune with corporate strategy and how to get the team members aligned with it. To implement their long-term vision, leaders needed to standardize and centralize responsibilities that for years had been decentralized. Many of their departments had administrative team members, but each of those employees completed steps of the same process differently. The inconsistency created confusion, waste, and extra work.

Hope was the right person to elevate this team to their next level. She submitted a plan for the new department's structure and the timeline for when it would roll out. Thankfully, the executive team approved it.

Hope and I spoke every two weeks. Even though she'd maintain her role as the CEO's assistant, her elevation with responsibility for a team of 20 was a daunting task. She decided to begin her new role by holding an expectations meeting with her new team. Hope was clear about what would not change and the small things that would change. She laid a strong foundation to ensure that each team member was clear about who was doing what, when, and how. For 99% of the employees on Hope's new team, the transition went smoothly. But there was one employee, Kathy, who was placed in a leadership role at her own request yet was not prepared for or a fit for the responsibility.

Kathy reported to Hope but didn't seem to want to be a leader to her new team members. Her DISC report, 12 Driving Forces, and core values confirmed that the role was out of alignment with who she was. She accepted the role because her previous boss wanted her to do it. So Hope spent an unreal amount of time coaching Kathy. It was a painful process for Hope as she repeatedly tried to uplift Kathy, but she was unable to make meaningful progress.

Remember, only help the people who want help.

As we navigated the centralization of tasks and standardized more processes, the team stayed true to their every-other-week meeting, they celebrated wins, they made sure they held one another accountable, and they clamped down on non-compliant behavior. Over time, Kathy reluctantly took more of Hope's counsel and she took less of Hope's time.

We started to see the administrative team members understand how the new team structure was benefiting them. Team members across multiple locations were learning new skills and were now able to complete tasks similar to their colleagues. The team became a peer-to-peer learning group. It became a fun, supportive exchange of knowledge and ideas where each person was helping another, finding new ways to serve.

Hope's high emotional intelligence allowed for her team to feel safe to frankly talk through challenging topics. Open discussions became the norm. Before, they worked in different departments using different processes to accomplish the same goal. If an employee was struggling with something at home, Hope was now able to offer that person the rest of the day off because she could redistribute the work to someone else. Her brand as a great leader—one who created psychological safety and helped each employee feel safe to be human and handle personal issues—solidified.

Placing an empathetic leader like Hope in change-centric situations is powerful. By choosing a leader who set clear expectations, communicated weekly, and allowed employees to make mistakes and learn from them, the team became engaged in a short time period. The team communicated in ways they hadn't before, and they more readily uplifted one another through challenging circumstances.

Your goal is the integration of employees' work and home lives into one deeply authentic and happy whole—to the benefit of both the individual and the organization.

How to Humanize Your Own Workplace

One of the most important jobs I do for organizations is help them design structures and systems for supporting employee growth and productive innovation. An organization I once supported rapidly acquired smaller businesses. During the buying spree, leaders did not invest time to define or implement a culture that would transcend and be adopted by the acquired businesses. So, office to office, employees behaved in accordance with the culture of their organization prior to it being acquired. I was asked to challenge leaders to design a cohesive organization-wide culture complete with an inspiring mission, easy-to-emulate core values, and reward systems that brought diverse team members together.

Each executive began looking at their work through fresh eyes and started having conversations they'd not had before. Thankfully, most rose to the challenge. We provided training that helped them see their corporate culture differently. We formed an "innovation team" that served as peer accountability for any leader who tried to uphold the old way of doing things. They were forced to set department and personal metrics-based goals that would be tied to their compensation for the first time in the org's history. We overtly rewarded leaders who were living by our new culture and had private conversations with those who weren't coming along fast enough. We encouraged early retirement and forced department heads to submit succession plans. With all of these actions, leaders realized that the culture was changing and they needed to get on board, as uncomfortable as the growth was for them.

They were willing to learn about the power of emotional connection. Emotions are literally contagious.[60] When organizations choose to not address the emotional makeup of and connection to the organization's purpose, there may be troubling effects:

- Distrust and poor communication
- Inefficient time management
- Slower and more costly processes
- Higher levels of disengagement and employee turnover
- Poor customer service and public brand

- Lower revenue and profit margin

When employees are discouraged from being emotional, human, or authentic, they'll likely become disengaged. These bullet points become the norm and happen at scale. The less human a business is, the higher the likelihood these effects will hinder it.

Entry level, repetitive skill jobs are being replaced by machine learning and artificial intelligence, and displaced workers are being forced to upskill.[61] Employees are being asked to learn, unlearn, and relearn at a pace humans have not encountered before. As a result, their brains' limbic systems are regularly entering the fight, flight, or freeze mode. As the barriers between work and home dissolve and increasing transparency brings personal issues into the workplace, organizational structures should be built to support employees—or companies may lose their talent.

So how can you make your organization more human?

1. Present a vision, long-term goals, and step-by-step plan to achieve a more human workplace. Often, an executive team takes responsibility for drafting, approving, and implementing mission and values statements, annual metrics-driven goals, and long-term vision. A more future-ready methodology would be to hold one-to-one meetings or focus groups across the organization to collect input from team members who interact with clients daily. Some will host an online idea forum or survey where all employees can participate in vision setting for the organization based on what they're experiencing day to day. When every employee's opinion is heard, they'll be more committed to the plan and work harder to ensure goals are achieved.

2. Adjust compensation, incentives, and bonus methodologies. The idea is to shift from a focus on solely rewarding accomplishing individual goals to rewarding employees for accomplishing individual and organizational goals concurrently. Those born into Generation Y view workplace success as a collaborative effort. They're at ease in teams, are achievement-oriented, and prefer to accomplish large goals with others. So ahead-of-their-time organizations that design in-the-moment incentives aligned with what they are trying to accomplish long term are greatly increasing their odds of success.

3. Develop mentorship and coaching frameworks. Leaders need tools, processes, and resources for helping employees manage communication conflict, rapid professional growth, and emotional workplace challenges. Organizations will have to mitigate the risks associated with employee emotions. Design structures for training more people inside your organization on how to support others' emotional circumstances. The goal is to create psychological safety for employees to be vulnerable and take risks. The era of outsourcing all mental health solutions is over.

4. Provide customized learning opportunities. There are four different learning styles: reading and writing, auditory, kinesthetic, and visual. Ideally, an organization would offer a variety of delivery methods for each specific learning objective—a book, a podcast, a video, a one-to-one coaching session, an offsite event, etc. The idea is to mass-customize and create an à la carte menu of ways a learning objective or skill can be absorbed by the employee. That's more challenging for the organization than simply offering a training and making attendance mandatory, but offering diversity is more effective. And, of course, more human.

5. Develop innovation feedback mechanisms. The book *Innovation to the Core* by Rowan Gibson and Peter Skarzynski reminds us that innovation is nothing more than a series of repeatable processes. When process-oriented employees see this, change becomes less scary. There's a blueprint to innovation. Invite every employee to participate through their annual goals, competitions, virtual suggestion boxes, innovation committees, compensation structures, and more. The likely outcome of doing so is a more engaged workplace, a new culture, and increased top-line revenue.

6. Bake appreciation into all events and facets of interaction. The way we combat the anxiety our employees feel is by deliberately offering more work-life integration, feedback, tailored coaching, and recognition for their effort. We need to ensure that younger employees feel seen and appreciated—weekly, in one-to-one and group meetings—for their growth and workplace contribution.

Humanizing the workplace will be hard. Engaging your workforce is hard. The pace of change in society is hard. These changes are happening, whether or not we like them, and expressing emotions at work isn't going to miraculously stop. So don't be on the wrong side of history. Returning to Age of Pisces mindsets and structures is no longer an option.

Grace in a Time of Great Change

Your parents aren't likely to understand your curriculum, your journey, as it is radically different than theirs. And that's okay. We can't control those around us. We have to release our expectations of them. We're here to learn from them. I believe everyone is doing the best they can in their lives with the information, experiences, and choices they have in front of them. Through society's awakening, a higher level of acceptance and understanding is coming. People will slowly begin to uplift one another as opposed to judging and tearing each other down.

As Noam Chomsky reminds us, "The smart way to keep people passive and obedient is to strictly limit the spectrum of acceptable opinion, but allow a very lively debate within that spectrum."[62]

For 100+ years, the range of debate and of acceptable conversation has been purposely limited. A small fraction of what's really happening on Earth is allowed to be discussed. As society transitions further into the Age of Aquarius, we're awakening to new ideas, technologies, ways of being, and more.

In 2020, we were asked to live life differently. We've been gifted the opportunity to reimagine every facet of our way of life. We began working at home. Our children attended school from home. We reconnected with our families. We adopted a slower pace of life. What this taught people is that they *can* change. It's safe to change. It's okay to change.

In the coming years, people will attempt personal change more, and they'll feel increasingly safe doing so. You'll learn you can accomplish bigger goals in untraditional ways. This book is designed to help you question society's norms and ways of life you want to move on from. Use these stories and processes to stay close to your Earth school curriculum. Anything is possible.

I often ask for grace as I've used these processes with so many people that I have the ability to see pieces of someone's future.

It's often far happier and more love-filled than their present. My challenge is that I want to help them create it tomorrow. Just because I believe in a person's possibilities and what I see coming for them doesn't mean I can speed it along. Their curriculum is theirs.

The more I experienced in this life, the more I realized just how much I changed who I was to fit into society. I've released the need to fit in and am working to create a more utopian world where authenticity is the norm.

Alan Watts, who brought Eastern philosophies to the West in the 1960s and 1970s, taught that the thing that matters most is the present moment. What you do for yourself now, emotionally and energetically, is the thing that creates the future.[63]

Holacracy

How teams are structured will look different in the near future. More organizations will adopt versions of holacracy as a management methodology.[64] Hierarchical business models are the traditional pyramid-shaped businesses where a CEO sits at the top and then each successive level of the organization has more and more people. A holacratic organization removes multiple levels of hierarchy and creates small work teams to accomplish goals. Power is redistributed from the top to every person organization-wide.

Employees choose their income, title, and projects they invest time into. It's a beautiful model of self-governance. As large hierarchies crumble, society will slowly begin grassroots empowerment of each person working. Some decisions will be made centrally, some locally. As these changes evolve in the workplace, it will be more important than ever to create and participate in small, engaged teams. Something that was once considered a "nice-to-have" soft skill (i.e., the ability to facilitate a team learning activity or coach your colleagues) will become crucial for thriving in the workplace in years to come.

Build a Culture of Coaching at Your Organization

I've been compared to performance coach Wendy Rhoades on *Billions*.[65] Wendy happens to be a fictional character created to inhabit a highly emotionally charged, over-the-top Showtime world. Her behavior can make coaches look more than a little morally dubious. But I like her character and the attention she draws to something I routinely do for companies: filling the role of staff psychologist and team performance coach.

Often, unhappy employees—even highly effective or high-producing ones—would simply quit if they found themselves struggling on a personal or professional level. Traditional human resources departments are reactive and compliance-based. They're designed to protect the company. Depending on the organization, they may help with recruitment, compensation, performance management, and more, but they're really charged with making sure staff follow rules. Most small- to medium-sized businesses haven't built human resources departments with proactive organizational development components to prepare employees for what's coming societally.

When an employee brings a personal, emotional, or family challenge to work, the HR department may default to calling the medical benefits provider's employee assistance program to help that employee get an appointment with a third-party therapist or psychologist. In my experience, this could take days, weeks, or even months.

Fortunately, that approach to supporting employees is changing. Executive coaches and staff psychologists are going mainstream as more organizations see the value of purposely investing in and developing their people. And preventing them from leaving when change appears. My work as a coach encompasses health, counseling, developmental techniques, industrial-organizational strategy, and social psychologist work to bolster the well-being of staff and keep the organization aligned with its vision.

Wendy Rhoades wants to make transformation happen *right now*; my goal is the integration of employees' work and home lives into one deeply authentic and happy whole—to the benefit of both the individual and the organization.

Generation Y recently became the largest percentage of the American workforce.[66] Because society has advanced so quickly, this generation doesn't have to worry about food, safety, or shelter. But as they move up Maslow's Hierarchy in search of their version of self-actualization, they'll routinely switch jobs if they have to. They're driven by a constant search for meaning. And I'm seeing this more with Generation X and some baby boomers. Ahead-of-their-time leaders are looking for ways to help their people develop within the context of their organization, to reduce crippling turnover and onboarding costs.

Organizations are realizing that to retain their most talented people, they need to take traditionally external benefits and have them exist internally—to deal with emotions and situations in the moment, on the spot.

Staff Coaching Topics

Coaching in the workplace may cover a myriad of topics. Here is a sample of some of the things I've worked with professionals on, both one-to-one and in group settings.

1. Emotional Intelligence: I work with personnel at all levels of an organization to build emotional intelligence. By reducing individuals' emotional reactivity to change and poor leadership communication, I help organizations reduce turnover and mitigate conflict. Because humans deeply dislike change bestowed upon them, I help companies be more transparent and involve their employees earlier when circumstances are shifting to achieve greater buy-in and even ownership of any change process.

2. Trauma: I examine childhood emotional trauma. By helping persons see how their adverse childhood experiences predict their behaviors later in life, I am able to help staff members break harmful patterns and perform at a more consistent level. I want to uncover the origin event of an adverse feeling so an individual can process and then safely release the emotion.

3. Time Management: Many employees struggle with staying focused on their strategic long-term goals in an environment with so many short-term demands and distractions. We look at their calendars. I give people the confidence to start saying "no" more often and "yes" to the requests or projects that are actually helping them accomplish their most meaningful goals.

4. Retention: By convincing employees who want to quit to stay, I routinely save organizations money. Turnover can cost companies 200% of a person's salary.[67] This number accounts for lost productivity, recruitment costs, temporary staff, training, and more. When you multiply that out, it can be one of the costliest line items an organization encounters each year.

5. Accountability: We are quick to place blame on our circumstances, surroundings, and our colleagues. I work to create personal accountability. When I ask tough questions of individuals, my goal isn't to ruffle feathers. Instead, I help persons to realize how they're complicit in creating the work conditions they say they don't want. From there, I help them walk into their personal power and stop blaming others. This exercise, when done throughout multiple departments, can change an organization's culture.

6. Values Examination: I perform the personal values exercise with each team member using the PEAK Values Card Deck, and connect those top six core values to the organization's values to find connection, purpose, and happiness.

7. Strategy: It's not good enough for an organization to just plan for the year ahead. By setting a long-term vision, your organization will avoid becoming the next Blockbuster. I challenge people to cut out activities, roles, and even entire departments not in alignment with a vision. When each employee has personal goals in alignment with shared long-term goals, synchronicity occurs across the functional boundaries of an organization. Employees think alike, support one another, and celebrate each step of the way.

8. Culture: Humans thrive in environments with rich cultures. We need stories to feel a connection to a cause bigger than our own. As such, I challenge leaders to think about the recognition systems, employee stories, wall art, meeting structures, leadership behaviors, and performance management activities that define culture. Don't let culture happen by accident. Create it with intention to attract and retain the best people.

Becoming Mainstream

In the time baby boomers were being raised, their parents were just coming out of World War II, after just coming out of the Great Depression. They were raised during a time when the refrain was "Just work, just work, just work." These individuals are, in their heart of hearts, emotional beings who want more than to just exist as productivity machines. But some of this cohort have suppressed that part of who they are. Gen X and Gen Y have endured significant struggles in the course of their childhoods and young adulthoods as well, from the shocking events of September 11, 2001, to the Great Recession years beginning in 2008 and 2009. But regardless of what challenges a generation has faced, there is value in sharing more of humanity in the workplace and helping our colleagues do the same.

There are no shortcuts when it comes to proactively developing your organization's people, but the good news is these sorts of exercises and processes that I've shared are slowly becoming mainstream. People now demand outlets to find personal meaning, and they need multiple ways to be engaged by their leader and employer.

Change often means loss. But after a loss has been processed emotionally, you may shift to a feeling of understanding and possibly even gratitude—a new appreciation for life. You reconsider and reorder priorities. You do something you've never done. You find joy in simpler things. Whatever route you're choosing, honor your feelings and grow to a place where you recognize how you're not the same person you were six months ago, how you generate value for others or are more aligned with your life's purpose.

I find ways to align a particular staff member's personal mission and journey with that of the organization. In this way, the employee can feel a sense of self-actualization while going to work each day, fully expressing the most authentic version of themself.

Key Takeaways

- Deepen relationships with your boss and colleagues.
- Reduce confusion by setting clear expectations and boundaries.
- To reduce stress, empower yourself and others by creating replicable systems.
- Only help people who genuinely want the help and are willing to do the work.
- Mistakes are not bad; they're learning experiences.
- Just like a virus, emotions are contagious.
- Employees have to learn, unlearn, and relearn at a pace never seen before.
- When employee opinions are used in the decision-making process, they'll be more committed and work harder to accomplish organizational goals.
- Best-in-class businesses don't outsource all mental health solutions.
- Innovation is nothing more than a series of processes repeated over a long period of time.
- 2020 taught people we can change. It's safe to change. It's okay to change.
- People deserve myriad ways to uncover personal meaning and to be engaged.
- Create cultures of recognition, praise, and celebration.

Chapter 9: Coach Yourself and Others

Leadership is about recognizing that there's a greatness in everyone, and your job is to create an environment where that greatness can emerge. ~Bill Campbell

I love seeing things come full circle.

A circle represents completion, a metaphor for the hero's journey, and the pain-to-purpose journey: you have a challenge, you overcome the challenge, and then you help other people overcome that challenge for themselves.[68] As I contemplate what's come full circle in my life, the first thing that popped into my mind was receiving the small nudges from the universe, repeatedly missing them, failing to be still. I was constantly acting, not having the courage to listen.

This got me to that point in early 2019 when the only nudge the universe seemed to have left was to get me to contemplate suicide.

My life, in the months leading up to that moment lying on the floor, was terribly uncomfortable. I was living in the studio apartment, my workshop series wasn't working, and I was investing money I didn't have into my business. Because I hadn't been still to receive and follow the universe's guidance, its message became so loud and so uncomfortable that I needed to be in the emotional place of wanting to not be here.

That was my learning: taking the step back and realizing there were numerous small nudges each step of my journey that I kept missing, didn't have the courage to hear, or purposely ignored. I needed to get to that moment of despair, that point of reflection to release the judgment I bestowed upon myself for not taking action when the universe's messages were soft.

Going through that experience meant life would come full circle and I'd likely help many other souls learn to recognize the small nudges. As people get to this phase of the process for themselves, the likelihood is old habits, rituals, and day-to-day structures they're accustomed to will be the things that stop them from hearing, noticing, and trusting the right next steps. What I *don't* want them to do is miss the little nudges the way I did.

In 2019, I repeatedly received messages that I should be saving money, relaxing, slowing down, and truly investing in myself and new relationships. In astrology, 2019 was for me a 6 year: a year designed to help you express love for yourself and for those close to you. Numerology is an ancient art that draws meaning, purpose, and guidance from numbers and number combinations. It is based upon a belief that the universe is a system, and at its core are numbers and the energies each represents. All things in the world can be dependent upon and can equate to numbers that offer new insights into your Earth school curriculum, personality traits, patterns, etc. Each base integer from 0–9 has a specific meaning and energy that offers insight into how you'll learn your lessons that day, month, or year.

Unfortunately, I ignored the messaging and doubled down on taking action not aligned with my curriculum. I chose the opposite of what I should have been doing and was forced to be still, find peace in silence, not do anything, and reflect on all of the events and experiences that led me to the point of suicide being a viable option.

Why did I choose to stay on Earth?

That was a big moment for me: finally releasing judgment of myself for my choices, for trying to be something I wasn't.

I believe strongly that all souls choose their parents before they come to Earth. I truly honor the blessings my parents bestowed upon me and the lessons they taught me. My father sent me to Scotland to play golf when I was 18, gifted me a Rolex when I was 22, and paid for my undergraduate degree. His love language is receiving and giving gifts, so it's no surprise he would express his love in those ways. Bringing my journey full circle involves me realizing that I chose him as a father for a purpose. My work is to understand, respect, and honor his journey through life—the hardships he endured, his curriculum, the actions he took to continue the family business when he may have wanted something different.

Three things he did *not* teach me—life was more than wealth, be available for your family, and the hours you worked didn't define you nor should be the ticket to the love you receive. In many ways, I only received the tip of the iceberg. I needed to experience not learning about employee engagement or respecting authenticity, so I would have a baseline to build my life from. What I needed to release over the last year was judgment.

All of the things I experienced as a child, adolescent, and young man I chose to do prior to coming to Earth. I chose to participate; I chose to learn. My father is an adult. He makes—every single day—conscious choices. I now choose to shed my judgment of his choices and honor the blessings he brought into my, my family's, and his employees' lives, and into the community. My curriculum has encompassed me refocusing on the blessings and optimistic pieces of his journey.

A moment of clarity in the past year was understanding my mother's journey a little more. She did the best she could, given the circumstances and the community around her. Instead of being frustrated with her for not finding a way to stand up to my dad or for not allowing me to be my authentic self, I wholeheartedly accept those experiences as core parts of my curriculum. I needed to feel what it was like to be a robot in someone else's business. I had to feel emotionally handcuffed to then know what it's like to be unbridled, free, and happy. The juxtaposition was required. Without it, I wouldn't have the courage to live authentically and aligned the way I do now.

Look at that parent, the one you tried really hard to receive love from when you were young, and let the frustration, anger, and sadness go. Release your judgment, your wishes, your expectations.

I had to learn that no matter how much action I take, there's no one who is going to love me the way I am capable of loving myself. There's no amount of work I do, no amount of money I make, no accomplishment that will replicate the feeling of love I feel for myself.

Self-love is not narcissism. It is not having a big ego. It is not instant gratification. It is having high regard for your own well-being and happiness. It means not sacrificing your well-being to please others. It means you accept your strengths and weaknesses as being key to how you're learning your curriculum. You nourish your body, brain, and soul. You appreciate and support your physical, psychological, and spiritual development. You prioritize yourself. Self-love will be different for everyone.

Love yourself. And help others love themselves. That's the only job.

Putting this into the context of the business world, it brings me joy we're developing an ecosystem of individuality, acceptance, and helping one another align. People are stepping into their own power personally and professionally. As a leader, having a deep and meaningful relationship with an employee or with a team is absolutely crucial. Your best people will leave if you're not in service of them and helping them walk into their authentic power. Because you've dealt with your own emotional baggage, you can now help others do the same. Coach yourself. Then coach others.

Creating Psychological Safety

So what does it mean to serve your people? It's really about creating one-to-one authentic connection and providing space for employees to feel psychologically safe. To help them find value in their voice. The employee who feels safe is the same employee who is going to feel free to share ideas, question groupthink, and open new revenue opportunities.

The concept comes down to this: What does a particular employee perceive the consequences to be of taking some risk? The risk could be as simple as making an unusual suggestion in a team meeting. Google's Project Aristotle found the internal teams that were the most productive were the ones who created a safe environment for every employee to offer risky alternatives or openly discuss learning from mistakes. They asked questions nobody else would ask, or offered new approaches nobody else was willing to offer.[69] In other words, these team members had, as Brené Brown teaches, the courage to be vulnerable.

In the recent Tim Ferriss podcast, "Lessons from a Trillion-Dollar Coach," listeners learned how Bill Campbell coached Eric Schmidt and a handful of executives at Google at the same time as he coached Steve Jobs and leaders at Apple. He created a way to develop a psychological safety between himself and the leaders of two competing companies and grow them both.[70]

It was Campbell's ability to create that sense of safety that made his coaching so effective.

Creating a culture of psychological safety is something you accomplish over time. Here is an idea you may find value in. By scheduling regular every-other-week one-to-one meetings with your direct reports and following these five steps in each meeting, you'll be well on your way to a more engaged team:

1. Recognition: Start a meeting by praising or delivering appreciation to your employee for an action or accomplishment. Take the time to find out how every individual on the team wants to receive appreciation, and deliver recognition in that way in each and every meeting.

2. Wins: Give your employee an opportunity to discuss what they feel were moments of accomplishment or things they did to take a big step toward a long-term goal. This could even be a new thing they learned you weren't aware of or maybe a personal accomplishment. The more time you spend at the beginning of a meeting having your direct report discuss wins, the more connected to you they will feel.

3. Actual Project Deliverables: What was it specifically they were supposed to complete in the last two weeks? Ask for a status update on the tasks they agreed to work on. This accountability matters. Make sure there's commitment and follow-through on important projects. Check in to see that next steps and deliverables are well aligned with the organization's strategic objectives as well as the individual's personal goals.

4. Challenges and Opportunities: Let's assume the employee is running into roadblocks or that people are hindering their progress. Your goal is to create an environment where they feel safe to ask you to remove a problem. Commit to doing something specific to help them by a specific date. If you can't remove the roadblock, you can help to brainstorm ways to get around or through the challenge.

5. Reflection and Goals: Openly talk through mistakes made and lessons learned. This is not something our society typically does, but it's a powerful tool in creating a learning environment. Then bring the meeting to a close by asking the employee to verbally share their metrics-based goals they'll accomplish before your next meeting.

You Are Already a Coach

A coach is a special kind of guide on our life's journey—someone who focuses on asking powerful how, what, and why questions. They believe the person they're working with is creative, resourceful, whole, and capable of finding their own answers to work and life challenges. A coach develops trust, a deep bond, and psychological safety to encourage vulnerability and calculated risk-taking. They create the environment for individual growth, purposeful action, and sustained improvement while maintaining privacy, confidentiality, and integrity.

There are many excellent formal coach training programs for those who wish to pursue this path professionally—I recommend looking into the International Coaching Federation—but in the meantime, I offer my advice here on what makes a great coach. No matter what your title happens to be, you can coach.

Best Coaching Practices

1. A coach has the emotional resilience to lovingly call you out when you're straying from your curriculum. A coach can see the best version of you and asks insightful questions to help you realign with that curriculum by recognizing and no longer repeating old patterns.

2. A coach judges no one. They improve *themself* and lead by example. A coach never stops learning.

3. A coach points out how all events are designed for our learning or our benefit. We cannot change the past, but we can change how we perceive and give meaning to it.

4. A coach can incorporate a discussion of adverse childhood experiences.[71] It is only by acknowledging and processing the traumas of our past that we move toward our future as lighter and freer versions of ourselves.

5. A coach believes humans are more similar than dissimilar and rapidly identifies patterns of behavior based on what he or she has observed in others.

6. A coach sees the consequences or downstream effects of decisions. A coach can talk through possible effects of an action to guide you to better outcomes in a shorter timeframe. I recently coached someone about three possible outcomes that may occur as a result of his owning up to questionable behavior. By talking through the consequences of all three, I helped him feel confident in proceeding with his plan and moving beyond his mistakes with his eyes wide open.

7. A coach manufactures learning experiences as words alone don't teach. A coach tries to avoid offering advice as it doesn't lead to lasting change. Instead, they help you learn by doing something new and reflecting on it. I recently had a client keep a pain journal for two weeks so she could see for herself the effects of her habits. The experience led her to make new choices about how she treated the people who worked for her. A pain journal can be quick one- to two-sentence bullet point entries that track who was involved, how events transpired, what was said, and how the person felt. After tracking for two weeks, we're likely to have 8–10 entries where we can identify patterns.

8. A coach notices when there is a disconnect in body language and chosen words. When you aren't being honest with yourself, a coach will notice. We rely on behavioral patterns and on intuition to get to the heart of the matter. A good coach notices when you are allowing fear to take you away from your curriculum.

9. A coach has firm boundaries. Boundaries help create and build trust. A good coach isn't an enabler. When you can trust your coach to tell you no, it helps you to feel safe to ask for what you want and need because resentment can't be built up. Also, as you talk about your triggers, it may trigger feelings in a coach. Thus, a good coach should have the ability to not take on others' stories.

If you're just beginning to coach, it is important you only coach on experiences you've encountered personally. By helping others overcome the same challenges you've overcome, you'll operate from a place of true alignment and integrity. People tend to trust people like themselves. Share your story openly. Create safe spaces for others to be vulnerable. No matter your background, your education, or your job title, you can coach yourself and others.

Finding Acceptance and Uplifting Others

The year 2020 introduced significant and lasting societal change. In this tumult, there is an opportunity to practice acceptance and to help others. The ancient Chinese philosopher Lao Tzu said, "Life is a series of natural and spontaneous changes. Don't resist them; that only creates sorrow. Let reality be reality."

By reflecting on your individual accomplishments, you realize that your next life phase can open even deeper levels of meaning. As you give back to and uplift others in the achievement of their goals, new learning and understanding occurs. When we help people overcome the same challenge we overcame in our younger years, the person we're helping mirrors back to us just how far we've come. We feel deeper levels of joy and accomplishment because we did what very few people have the courage to do: live not in accordance with society's mores, but instead live our Earth school curriculum no matter the judgment or shame bestowed upon us by others.

An awakened soul begins to realize just how connected it is to everything around itself, that the universe is always communicating to you if you're quiet enough to hear the messages. When you've reached this level, you release the need to control outcomes, and you become able to act without expectation of return. From this place, you nourish the advancement of those around you and finally accept that the denigration of one soul is a denigration of the entire ecosystem.

Thus, it's our responsibility to awaken ourselves so we can guide others through their awakening.

After a soul chooses a set of parents and its human body, it passes through the veil of illusion effectively forgetting everything in its long history. In human form, as the person ages, its goal is to remember its soul's actual purpose, the true nature of earth and energy, and how we're all connected by serving as mirrors for one another. Although our physical bodies are apart, we are connected by electromagnetic links our human eyes can't see. By honoring one another's journeys, we honor our own progress, lessons to be learned, and the meaning of our time on Earth.

Release Judgment

The second lesson of best coaching practices above reminds us not to judge. Have you felt yourself judging others lately? Are they "doing" this time in history wrong? Are they believing the wrong things, according to your view of the world? Or taking what you perceive to be wrong actions? A coach respects everyone's pain-to-purpose journey and sees themself in others. When you feel judgmental, take these steps to release your emotion.

1. Recognize your limbic system response: You'll do anything you can to protect yourself. When you feel a strong emotion, your limbic system is triggered and your body will go into fight, flight, or freeze mode. The best thing to do is nothing. Take a step back. Don't say anything. You won't regret pausing.

2. Ask, "What is their pain?": This question offers others the benefit of the doubt. All emotional reactivity today is due to a previous unhealed wound. If someone says or does something you feel is inappropriate, try to remember they're being confronted with old, unhealed emotions. It's powerful to consider, "What's the origin story of this?"

3. Find the good: All persons have good qualities. We need to uncover and remind ourselves of them—and when we do, we feel better ourselves because we can imagine that others will give *us* the benefit of the doubt as well. Peace begets peace. It's easy to judge someone based on how we perceive their personality or character. A coach instead considers situational factors affecting that person's choices.

4. Realize we are all more similar than dissimilar: With all humans you interact with, ask, "What do I share in common with this person?" We all want to be trusted; we all want to be respected. Society teaches us to look for differences, but it's more beneficial to look for commonalities.

5. Look in the mirror: Are you placing judgment on an action that has previously left you with regret? When we haven't forgiven ourselves, that wound can manifest itself as judgment of others. It's time to tell a new story and release the old weight.

Growth happens through adversity. Humans have had many reasons to judge one another. But if you would like to make something better out of your experience, you absolutely can. What are those things you've learned about yourself? What do you want to shed and leave behind? You have time to do something new right now.

All the answers to life's most pressing questions are already inside you. Freedom, choice, feeling heard, and the ability to do what you want is foundational to loving life.

The Benefits of Change

In many organizations today, baby boomers are resistant to implementing change and breaking down the hierarchies they helped to build. However, Generation X and Generation Y leaders are advancing a little each day in bringing the Age of Aquarius into the mainstream. Matrixed teams and grassroots efforts are winning favor, which is why team coaching is the final step in my overall process. It creates self-actualization: achieving one's full potential and accomplishing everything one can. A coach helps us do this for ourselves, and then we can coach others to do the same.

Team coaching also leads to more individual contribution. Belonging to a cause bigger than your own leads to serving and focusing on helping and supporting others. There's more to Earth than the material world, and by engaging in this process, people come to feel that materialism holds less value. It becomes easier and more possible to make the world a better place than the one you were born into. Coaches believe the protégé has all the answers inside themself, so a team of coaches coaching one another is an ecosystem of people who push one another to be the best they can be, to align with their path quickly, and to deepen their levels of self-trust. Thus, in shedding old individualistic, self-focused, Age of Pisces versions of ourselves, we bring things full circle by realizing how connected everything is.

Once we have awakened to our life's true purpose, the next step is to help others awaken. The whole ecosystem begins awakening, the energy on Earth rises, the Schumann resonance (Earth's heartbeat) rises. Our work is not done until every single human KNOWS the answer is inside them, that every single person feels appreciated, lives up to their potential, is in control of where they distribute time, is aligned with their curriculum. When we coach one another, we rapidly identify our soul family, we see life's challenges as the path, and we build emotional resilience.

Forward-thinking executive teams are actively seeking input from employees and stakeholders at all levels of the organization. When employees are sent to third-party training to teach them best practices, goals are achieved more quickly and with less conflict. A trend of certifying employees as coaches allows everyone in an organization to get feedback twice as much and twice as fast. Finally, a big change to organizational culture is the advent of widespread work-from-home policies.

How will society benefit from all of this change? Relationships will be filled with trust, respect will be shown to others even when disagreements occur, win-win resolution will become the norm, and people will be encouraged to learn experientially. Making mistakes will be okay, vulnerable conversations will become the norm, calculated risk-taking will be celebrated, and people will release childhood traumas. We will learn processes and systems to advance both spiritually and emotionally and find deeply meaningful ways to contribute to society.

I'm not inspired by perfection, athletes, celebrities, business leaders, or people who project the image of success. I am inspired by everyday people who openly share their imperfections, life's ups and downs, and how they're working to better their lives.

Whatever your situation, our current time in the flow of history is intentionally hitting a reset button on the areas of your life you were previously unhappy. You've been given a window of time to reflect, to pinpoint areas of focus, and to shed what doesn't elevate you to your life's next level.

If you're clear that you're ready, and are open to experiential learning, now is an ideal time to confidently walk forward into the future you've been thinking about.

Key Takeaways

- Help other people take ownership and remove blame and excuses.
- See your own soul and not simply your human body.
- In each step of your journey, the universe will present you with several small nudges to align with your curriculum. Don't miss them.
- Your soul chooses its curriculum prior to being born as human.
- Internal peace is yours when you shed the desire to continually judge others because their choices are different than yours.
- No one will ever love you the way you're capable of loving yourself.
- Psychological safety is born out of workplaces that allow individuality and purposely help others align with their curriculum.
- Coaches are not mentors, counselors, or consultants; they focus on asking how, what, and why questions.
- Judge no one.
- All circumstances are designed for our benefit.
- As you awaken and lead by example, others will feel empowered to follow in your footsteps.

Conclusion

The only way to make sense out of change is to plunge into it, move with it, and join the dance. ~Alan Watts

In August 2020, Tiffany and I visited my family in Michigan. We rented a home a little more than two hours north of where I was raised. My mom, dad, sister, brother-in-law, niece, and nephew spent the weekend with us.

It was one of my life's most fulfilling experiences.

I felt complete, knowing my family was a conduit to learning my life's curriculum. I felt at peace and joy being with them.

I felt as though my life had come full circle. Just two years prior, I contemplated how I'd leave Earth early. In Northern Michigan, I felt an unbreakable connection to completing my life's mission.

Two years ago, my efforts to expand my coaching practice fell flat. In 2020, I slowed down, listened to the universe, and was guided to projects that were beyond fruitful and gratifying.

I used to sleep alone in a 600-square-foot apartment in one of Phoenix's toughest neighborhoods. In 2020, I sleep soundly next to Tiffany in a beautiful home in a quiet North Phoenix neighborhood.

I used to wonder if I'd ever be worthy of love. Today, Tiffany delivers words of affirmation verbally, via text, and in cards she gifts me. I feel unconditionally loved.

In Glen Arbor on a cloudy day, my dad, brother-in-law, nephew, and I went golfing. It was the first time three generations of Seavers played together.

Tiffany and I bought white chef's hats, my sister brought permanent markers, and we held a competition to see who could best decorate their hat. A buffet of sauces and pizza toppings awaited everyone to custom create whatever pizza they desired.

On a sunny Sunday, my family rented a boat and cruised Glen Lake. My niece and nephew loved being pulled behind the boat. My mom and Tiffany soaked up the sun. I jumped off the boat repeatedly and swam in the lake's crystal-clear waters.

Each night, I slipped into bed with a calm I'd never experienced with my family before. My emotional traumas were shed. My need to judge and correct disappeared. My desire to be something I wasn't to fit in was replaced with a knowing that I was exactly where I needed to be.

In the past year, I've seen my business transform for the better as well. It has manifested in:

- Increased connection to clients due to this process
- Clients seeing amplified results thanks to this work
- Clients willing to take on the work to become authentic and reap the benefits
- Deepening and expanding the growth for clients, with them seeing measurable results

I am also happy to report that the one thing that has *not* changed in my life is Cleopatra: she is still the special independent cat and evolved soul she's always been.

Each of the individuals whose stories I shared—Avni, Sara, Nick, Crystal, Luke, Aleah, Hope, and others—did the hard, emotional work. They aligned with their Earth school curriculum. They began giving back to their community in some way. Individuals in those communities are now receiving help from them. And those people are paying it forward. It creates this endless cycle of uplifting one another.

Our society was designed to distribute human energy for the purpose of the accumulation of wealth. It was a very purposely created and well-orchestrated system. That system has been broken. There is nothing wrong with material wealth and possessions; it is our attachment to them that leaves us out of alignment. It is okay to desire material wealth; yet if that is the focus, your soul loses most every time. Use prosperity to give.

What I want you to do in the months that follow reading this book is release what you learned in the previous 30 or 40 years of your life. Daily, move 1% closer to your actual life's curriculum in a way that feels peaceful. You don't have to take constant action.

You don't have to compare yourself to anybody else. You don't have to emulate a celebrity or business person. Look in the mirror and say, "I chose to come to Earth this time to learn this lesson. And I'm doing so beautifully, authentically, individualistically on my own."

Wake up and feel a sense of calmness that you are exactly where you are supposed to be at this moment in time.

When you have the capability to shed old emotions and not be triggered by things that used to trigger you, you are well on your way. When you can control your energy and hold things lightly, you'll know you've made significant progress.

That's the real purpose of life, not having material possessions. They don't matter; they were a means to an end in the old version of society.

Spend time in nature.

Nurture your relationships.

Find happiness in the most basic things.

I know that the transition from the Age of Pisces to the Age of Aquarius has been challenging, and 2020 was the worst year. It brought tremendous pain to the surface. In the coming years, people will learn why society was designed the way it was and begin to understand why so many people led lives that were disconnected from their souls' work, their curriculum.

I have such a strong connection to and belief in the pureness of humanity. It gives me confidence that we are all going to be just fine.

Have faith . . . in you.

Things are always working out for you.

You've arrived at *I Know*, and you're never going back.

Notes

[1] Bridges transition model. (n.d.). https://wmbridges.com/about/what-is-transition/. Accessed June 16, 2020.

[2] H. R. Hulnick & M.R. Hulnick. (2013). *Loyalty to your Soul: The heart of spiritual psychology.* Carlsbad, CA: Hay House.

[3] The mere exposure effect. (2016, March 15). http://socialpsychonline.com/2016/03/the-mere-exposure-effect/. Accessed June 16, 2020.

[4] Principles of persuasion. (n.d.). https://www.influenceatwork.com/principles-of-persuasion/. Accessed June 16, 2020.

[5] S. Kamrath & B. Lipton. (2012, February 7). Happy health child: A holistic approach: An interview with Bruce Lipton. *Bruce H. Lipton, PhD* [personal website]. https://www.brucelipton.com/resource/article/happy-healthy-child-holistic-approach. Accessed June 16, 2020.

[6] Editors of Encyclopedia Britannica. (n.d.). Precession of the equinoxes. *Encyclopedia Britannica.* https://www.britannica.com/science/precession-of-the-equinoxes. Accessed June 16, 2020.

[7] The complete guide to how the precession of the equinoxes work. (2019, February 21). https://medium.com/@humanoriginproject/the-complete-guide-to-how-precession-of-the-equinoxes-work-738b099a15a6. Accessed June 16, 2020.

[8] M. E. P. Seligman. (n.d.). https://ppc.sas.upenn.edu/people/martin-ep-seligman. Accessed June 16, 2020.

[9] C. Moore. (2020, December 10). Learned optimism: Is Martin Seligman's glass half full? *PositivePsychology.com.* https://positivepsychology.com/learned-optimism/. Accessed June 16, 2020.

[10] Schumann resonance. (n.d.). https://www.nasa.gov/mission_pages/sun-earth/news/gallery/schumann-resonance.html. Accessed June 16, 2020.

[11] J. Clear. (2018). *Atomic habits: An easy & proven way to build good habits & break bad ones.* New York: Penguin Publishing Group.

[12] P. Coelho. (2014). *The alchemist.* 25th Anniversary Edition. New York: HarperCollins.

[13] The hero with a thousand faces, by Joseph Campbell. (n.d.). https://www.jcf.org/works/titles/the-hero-with-a-thousand-faces/. Accessed June 16, 2020.

[14] Tanaaz. (n.d.). The 5 soul groups you belong to. *Forever Conscious.* https://foreverconscious.com/5-soul-groups-belong. Accessed June 19, 2020.

[15] B. Brown. (2012). *Daring greatly.* New York, NY: Penguin Random House.

[16] Hulnick & Hulnick. (2013).

[17] N. Burton. (2016, January 7). What are basic Emotions? *Psychology Today.* https://www.psychologytoday.com/us/blog/hide-and-seek/201601/what-are-basic-emotions. Accessed June 16, 2020.

[18] S. J. Ashford & D. S. DeRue. (2012). Developing as a leader: The power of mindful engagement. *Organizational Dynamics, 41,* 146–154. http://webuser.bus.umich.edu/sja/pdf/DevAsLeader.pdf. Accessed June 17, 2020.

[19] B. Brennan & J. A. Smith. (1988). *Hands of light: A guide to healing through the human energy field.* New York: Bantam.

[20] K. Truman (2005). *Feelings buried alive never die.* St. George, UT: Olympus Distributing.

[21] Preventing adverse childhood experiences. (2020, April 3). https://www.cdc.gov/violenceprevention/aces/fastfact.html. Accessed June 17, 2020.

[22] Generational differences chart. (2017). http://www.wmfc.org/uploads/GenerationalDifferencesChartUpdated2017.pdf. Accessed June 17, 2020.

[23] J. Vitale & I. H. Len. (2007). *Zero limits: The secret Hawaiian system for wealth, health, peace, and more.* Hoboken, NJ: John Wiley & Sons.

[24] Dr. Shefali. https://drshefali.com/. Accessed June 17, 2020.

[25] TTI Success Insights. https://www.ttisi.com/. Accessed August 14, 2020.

[26] Hulnick & Hulnick (2013).

[27] Why we hate in others what we hate in ourselves. (n.d.). https://www.yoga-anatomy.com/why-we-hate-in-others-what-we-hate-in-ourselves/. Accessed July 2, 2020.

[28] Why TTI? (n.d.). https://www.ttisi.com/why-tti/. Accessed July 2, 2020.

[29] What is DiSC®? Deepen your understanding of yourself and others. (n.d.). https://www.discprofile.com/what-is-disc/overview/. Accessed July 1, 2020.

[30] https://12drivingforces.ttisi.com/. Accessed August 14, 2020.

[31] 12 driving forces®: What does work mean to you? (n.d.). https://12drivingforces.ttisi.com/. Accessed July 1, 2020.

[32] PEAK Values® Card Deck. (n.d.). https://www.thepeakfleet.com/product/peak-values-core-values-card-deck/. Accessed August 14, 2020.

[33] PEAK Values® Card Deck. (n.d.).

[34] C. McChesney, S. Covey, & J. Huling. (2012). *The 4 disciplines of execution: Achieving your wildly important goals.* New York, NY: Free Press.

[35] Schumann resonance. (n.d.).

[36] Medicine Cards. https://medicinecards.com/. Accessed August 14, 2020.

[37] M. Sol. (2019.) Synchronicity, symbolism, and the meaning of numbers. *Lonerwolf.* https://lonerwolf.com/meaning-of-numbers/. Accessed November 2, 2020.

[38] R. Bruce. (2009). *The complete book of out-of-body experiences.* Newburyport, MA: Hampton Roads Publishing.

[39] Boulder Longevity Institute. https://boulderlongevity.com/. Accessed August 14, 2020.

[40] Dream Moods. https://www.dreammoods.com. Accessed Oct. 8, 2020.

[41] Life purpose calculator. (n.d.). https://www.peacefulwarrior.com/life-purpose-calculator/. Accessed August 14, 2020.

[42] M. Hall. (2019, May 7). Ruling planets of the zodiac signs. *Liveabout.com.* https://www.liveabout.com/ruling-planets-of-the-zodiac-signs-4686674. Accessed August 14, 2020.

[43] Emotional Intelligence and the EQ Assessment: What You Need to Know. (2020, July 9). https://blog.ttisi.com/emotional-intelligence-and-the-eq-assessment-what-you-need-to-know. Accessed November 2, 2020.

[44] Emotional intelligence and the EQ assessment: What you need to know.

[45] Ibid.

[46] Ibid.

[47] Ibid.

[48] Ibid.

[49] Valley Leadership. https://www.valleyleadership.org/. Accessed August 14, 2020.

[50] Generational differences chart. (2017).

[51] Retiring the generation gap: How employees young and old can find common ground, by Jennifer J. Deal. (2007). https://www.wiley.com/en-us/Retiring+the+Generation+Gap%3A+How+Employees+Young+and+Old+Can+Find+Common+Ground-p-9780787988654. Accessed August 14, 2020.

[52] The four stages of life according to Carl Jung. (n.d.). https://fractalen-lightenment.com/48063/life/the-four-stages-of-life-according-to-carl-jung. Accessed October 7, 2020.

[53] J. A. Howard (2000). Social psychology of identities. *Annual Review of Sociology*, *26*, 367–9. http://www.uvm.edu/pdodds/teaching/courses/2009-08UVM-300/docs/others/2000/howard2000a.pdf Accessed November 2, 2020.

[54] InsightTimer. https://insighttimer.com/. Accessed October 8, 2020.

[55] Principles of persuasion. (n.d.).

[56] EverythingPeople This Week! (n.d.). *ASE*. https://www.aseonline.org/News/EverythingPeople-This-Week/ArtMID/543/ArticleID/1686/Is-an-8-hour-Work-Day-Productive. Accessed August 14, 2020.

[57] A. C. Keller, L. L. Meier, A. Elfering, & N. K. Semmer. (2019, February 15). Please wait until I am done! Longitudinal effects of work interruptions on employee well-being. *An International Journal of Work, Health & Organizations*, *34*(2), 148–67. https://www.tandfonline.com/doi/full/10.1080/02678373.2019.1579266. Accessed August 14, 2020.

[58] J. Ray. (2019, April 25). Americans' stress, worry and anger intensified in 2018. *Gallup*. https://news.gallup.com/poll/249098/americans-stress-worry-anger-intensified-2018.aspx. Accessed August 14, 2020.

[59] Appreciation at Work. https://www.appreciationatwork.com. Accessed Oct. 13, 2020.

[60] S. Barsade & F. Klotz. (2019, November 6). Employee emotions aren't noise—They're data. *MITSloan*. https://sloanreview.mit.edu/article/employee-emotions-arent-noise-theyre-data/. Accessed Oct. 8, 2020.

[61] V. S. Ratcheva & T. Leopold. (2018, September 17). 5 things to know about the future of jobs. *World Economic Forum*. https://www.weforum.org/agenda/2018/09/future-of-jobs-2018-things-to-know/. Accessed Oct. 8, 2020.

[62] C. Galapon. (2019, March 31). Noam Chomsky quote: What does it mean? *Lean Agile Guru*. https://leanagileguru.com/2019/03/31/noam-chomsky-quote-what-does-it-mean-in-the-lean-agile/. Accessed August 4, 2020.

[63] M. Popova. (2014, January 27). The ego and the universe: Alan Watts on becoming who you really are. *BrainPickings*. https://www.brainpick-ings.org/2014/01/27/alan-watts-taboo/. Accessed August 4, 2020.

[64] Holacracy. https://www.holacracy.org/. Accessed August 14, 2020.

[65] N. McAlone. (2018, June 11). "Billions" star Maggie Siff on how Tony Robbins helped her prep, and why her character feels like a "big cosmic joke." *Business Insider*. https://www.businessinsider.com/billions-star-maggie-siff-says-tony-robbins-helped-craft-character-of-wendy-rhoades-2018-6. Accessed August 14, 2020.

[66] R. Fry. (2018, April 11). Millennials are the largest generation in the U.S. labor force. *Pew Research Center.* https://www.pewresearch.org/fact-tank/2018/04/11/millennials-largest-generation-us-labor-force/. Accessed August 14, 2020.

[67] The hidden cost of employee turnover. (2016, October 6). https://online.alvernia.edu/articles/cost-employee-turnover/. Accessed Oct. 8, 2020.

[68] M. S. Seaver. (2018, July 3). The pain-to-purpose journey. *Michael. S. Seaver.* https://michaelsseaver.com/leadership/the-pain-to-purpose-journey/. Accessed Oct. 8, 2020.

[69] Guide: understand team effectiveness. (n.d.). https://rework.with-google.com/print/guides/5721312655835136/. Accessed August 14, 2020.

[70] E. Schmidt. (2019, April 14). Lessons from a trillion-dollar coach—The Tim Ferriss Show. *Podcast Notes.* https://podcastnotes.org/2019/04/14/schmidt/. Accessed August 14, 2020.

[71] About the CDC-Kaiser ACE study. (2020, April 13). https://www.cdc.gov/violenceprevention/acestudy/about.html. Accessed August 14, 2020.

CPSIA information can be obtained
at www.ICGtesting.com
Printed in the USA
LVHW011122210121
676969LV00003B/306